A JOURNEY OF ENTREPRENEURIAL INSPIRATION

**A Guide to
Building America's Finest Business in San Diego**

VASQUEZ

Scaling Leadership

For information, address MV Consulting Publisher, 374 East H Street, A133, Chula Vista, CA 91910.

This book may be purchased for education, business, or sales promotional use. For information, please email me@miguelvasquez.com

First edition: ISBN 979-8-218-31845-1

As I sit down to pen this foreword, my mind races back to the vibrant streets of my hometown in Mexico. As an immigrant, I carry with me the spirit of resilience, determination, and the undying passion for entrepreneurship that flows through my veins. It is with deep admiration that I reflect on the creators of economic vitality and the architects of economic development who have shaped our world.

The path from an idea to innovation has always fascinated me. Witnessing the transformative power of entrepreneurship firsthand, I have come to realize its immense potential to change lives, communities, and even entire nations. This awe-inspiring journey has ignited a fire within me and driven my unwavering commitment to empowering aspiring entrepreneurs on their path to success.

Throughout my career, I have been fortunate enough to work closely with thousands of young and ambitious entrepreneurs, each with a dream to leave their mark on the world. Their unwavering determination, coupled with my humble guidance and support, has yielded incredible results. Seeing their dreams take shape and witnessing the impact they create in their communities has been the ultimate reward, filling my heart with a sense of purpose and fulfillment.

I have come to understand that entrepreneurship is not just about creating profitable ventures; it is about transforming lives, fostering innovation, and creating opportunities for others. It is about paving the way for the next generation of change-makers, empowering them to overcome challenges, and guiding them toward a future of boundless possibilities.

In the face of adversity, I have seen entrepreneurs rise, armed with resilience, creativity, and a relentless drive to

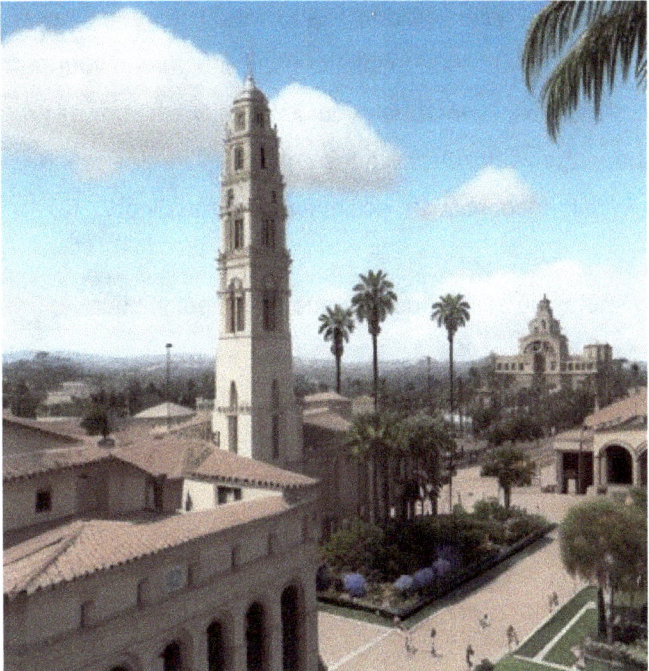

succeed. Their stories of triumph against all odds continue to inspire me, reminding me that every dream is valid and that anything is achievable with the right support and guidance.

This book is a testament to the transformative power of entrepreneurship, the unbreakable spirit of immigrants, and the incredible impact that we can make when we come together to nurture and uplift the dreams of young visionaries.

So, to all the entrepreneurs, dreamers, and innovators who dare to defy the odds, this forward is for you. May it serve as a beacon of inspiration, guiding you on your path to greatness. Remember, your ideas have the power to shape the world, and with the right passion, dedication, and guidance, you can achieve the extraordinary.

Wishing you all the success and fulfillment in your entrepreneurial life.

With Gratitude and Optimism,

Miguel D. Vasquez

Dedicated to SPD

Table of Contents

INTRODUCTION: A JOURNEY OF ENTREPRENEURIAL INSPIRATION... 8

CHAPTER 1: PLANNING AND RESEARCH.. 13

CHAPTER 2: LEGAL CONSIDERATIONS.. 30

CHAPTER 3: BUILDING A STRONG BRAND 43

CHAPTER 4: DEVELOPING YOUR PRODUCTS OR SERVICES........ 56

CHAPTER 5: SALES AND MARKETING STRATEGIES...................... 69

CHAPTER 6: DELIVERING EXCEPTIONAL CUSTOMER SERVICE .. 93

CHAPTER 7: OPERATIONAL EFFICIENCY AND PRODUCTIVITY .. 104

CHAPTER 8: HUMAN RESOURCES AND RISK MITIGATION.......... 115

CHAPTER 9: FINANCIAL PRO FORMA 129

CHAPTER 10: SMALL BUSINESS LENDING AND GRANTS 139

CHAPTER 11: USING ACCOUNTING SOFTWARE 158

APPENDIX A: SAMPLE BUSINESS PLAN TEMPLATE 172

APPENDIX B: STARTUP COST EXPENSES 176

APPENDIX C: HIRING AND ONBOARDING CHECKLIST................. 178

APPENDIX D: MARKETING PLAN TEMPLATE.................................. 180

APPENDIX E: CUSTOMER SERVICE SCRIPTS & TEMPLATES...... 182

APPENDIX F: RESEARCH AND INDUSTRY ARTICLES................... 184

APPENDIX G: SBDC SITES 185

Introduction: A Journey of Entrepreneurial Inspiration

In the bustling streets of San Diego, a city that has shaped my love for entrepreneurship, I have found a deep kinship with every startup and founder who dares to dream big. As an immigrant from Mexico, my personal journey and experiences have shaped my perspective and ignited a deep appreciation for the entrepreneurial spirit and the transformative power of hard work and determination.

With a degree in business administration from the prestigious University of San Diego, I embarked on a path that allowed me to explore every facet of business management. From finance to marketing, operations to strategy, I developed a passion for understanding how businesses operate and thrive. It was during my time at the university that I began to appreciate the transformative power of entrepreneurship and the awe-inspiring path from a simple idea to an innovative solution.

Over the years, I had the privilege of holding managerial and executive leadership positions across various industries. These experiences taught me to recognize the importance of building coalitions and fostering collaborations that lead to joint success. Witnessing the impact that can be achieved when diverse minds come together with a common purpose further solidified my belief in the power of collective growth.

However, it was my role in helping thousands of young entrepreneurs reach their dreams that truly provided a profound purpose in my career. Guiding them through the intricacies of starting and scaling their ventures, I witnessed their unwavering dedication, creativity, and resilience. Their journeys became intertwined with my own, fueling my passion for fostering an entrepreneurial ecosystem where innovation thrives, and dreams become reality.

First and foremost, let me express my deep admiration for the boundless entrepreneurial spirit. It's like a magical potion that infuses passion, creativity, and a relentless drive to make things happen. Whether you're a seasoned startup founder or just dipping your toes into the startup waters, you are part of a remarkable tribe that dares to dream big, disrupt the status quo, and rewrite the rules of the game.

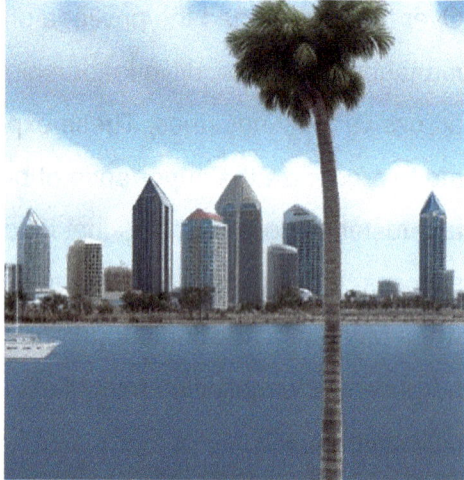

Now, let's talk about San Diego—the enchanting city that has left an indelible mark on my entrepreneurial soul. With its sun-kissed beaches, laid-back vibes, and thriving startup ecosystem, San Diego exudes a unique blend of inspiration and innovation. It's a place where ideas come alive, and dreams turn into reality. From the bustling streets of Gaslamp Quarter to the tech hubs in Sorrento Valley, this city fuels the fires of entrepreneurship and nurtures the spirit of collaboration.

At a very early stage of my career, I quickly realized that there's more to entrepreneurship than just crunching numbers and drafting business plans. It's about embracing the joy in the day, celebrating small victories, and not taking ourselves too seriously. Because let's face it, business can be a wild rollercoaster ride, and laughter is the best antidote to the inevitable twists and turns along the way.

This guide is not intended to be all-inclusive, but rather, a source to point you in the right direction. You can begin in any chapter, but it is recommended that you start from the top. So, dear reader, in the spirit of keeping things light and lively, I pledge to sprinkle some humor, injecting smiles and chuckles into our

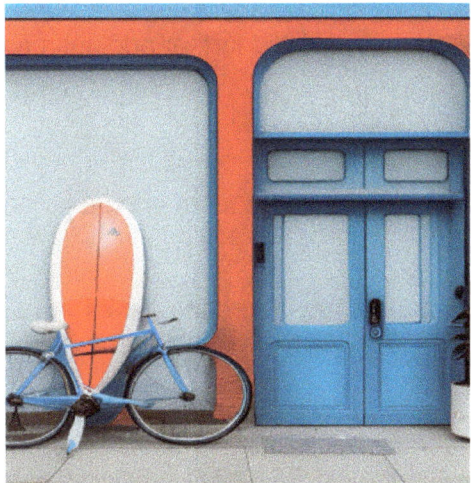

entrepreneurial escapade. Prepare yourself for a delightful mix of business insights, witty anecdotes, and, of course, some side-splitting jokes that will keep you entertained and inspired. Well, at least my kids thought they were funny.

Laughter is not just a fleeting moment of amusement; it's a powerful tool that connects us, ignites our creativity, and reminds us to find joy in every step of the entrepreneurial dance. So, let's lace up our entrepreneurial shoes, put on our humor hats, and join this adventure together, forging lasting connections, and making memories that will leave us smiling long after the final page is turned.

And now, without further ado, let me tickle your funny bone with a joke:

Why did the sales team bring a ladder to the bar?

Because they heard the drinks were on the house!

Cheers to entrepreneurship and good laughs!

Chapter 1: Planning and Research

In the realm of entrepreneurship, we often hear the timeless saying, "If you fail to plan, you plan to fail." It's a reminder that without a solid business model and plan in place, the path to success can be fraught with obstacles and uncertainty. But what if we look at planning not just as a safeguard against failure, but as a path toward creating joyful memories and a lasting legacy?

Imagine a time of family, where laughter filled the air, and moments of triumph became the fabric of our lives. As I reflect on my own entrepreneurial journey, I am reminded of the lessons imparted by my grandfather, a resilient and determined man who faced countless challenges but never

wavered in his pursuit of success.

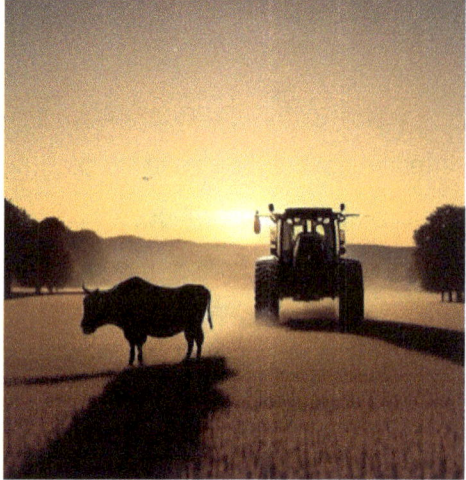

My grandfather, a humble farmer, understood the true value of time and love. He knew that to secure a prosperous future for his family, he had to meticulously plan and execute his business model. He was a constant mover, a doer, always working and figuring out the next steps to ensure his family's success.

With every seed he planted, he envisioned the bountiful harvest it would yield. Although he did not write a business plan, he planned a roadmap to prosperity, a testament to his unwavering commitment. Through his dedication and foresight, he not only achieved financial success but also handed down wealth to generations of family farmers, creating a legacy that continues to thrive today.

Remember, dear reader, that the way toward building a successful business is not just about the destination but also the moments we cherish along the way. Let us embark on this chapter with the spirit of my grandfather, driven by a passion for growth, an unwavering work ethic, and the understanding that planning is the key that unlocks the doors to our dreams.

From Ideation to Innovation: Unleashing the Power of the Entrepreneurial Spirit:

Welcome to the exciting world of small business planning and research! In this chapter, you will need to take the reins and launch the process of laying the foundation for your entrepreneurial success. So grab your notepad and let's plunge into the world of planning and research, San Diego style!

Defining Your Business Idea:

Every successful business starts with a brilliant idea, like the sun-kissed beaches of San Diego. To launch your entrepreneurial venture, it is crucial to define and refine your business idea, identify your target audience, and uncover the unique value you bring to the market. Whether you dream of opening a trendy coffee shop in North Park or a surfboard rental service in Pacific Beach, transforming your idea into a winning proposition is in your hands.

Conducting Market Research:

Just as surfers study the ocean swells, understanding your market is essential for navigating the business landscape. Equipping yourself with the tools to conduct effective market research, analyze industry trends, explore customer preferences, and study your competitors becomes vital. With a deep understanding of the San Diego market, you'll be able to ride the waves of demand and deliver products and services that resonate with the local community.

Equip Yourself with the Right Tools:

You will need the right tools to navigate the waters of market research, so equip yourself with data-driven knowledge. From online surveys and focus groups to data analytics and customer interviews, these tools will be your trusted companions in uncovering valuable insights about your target audience. Embrace technology, harness the power of social media, and explore market research platforms to gather the data and information that will steer your business decisions.

Analyze Industry Trends like a Pro:

In the dynamic business landscape of San Diego, staying ahead requires analyzing industry trends, understanding the local market, networking strategically, and making informed moves. So, equip yourself with the knowledge, connections, and insights necessary to ride the waves of success and make strategic moves that propel your business forward in San Diego's vibrant entrepreneurial ecosystem.

- **Local Industry Publications:** Stay updated on San Diego's business scene by following local industry publications such as San Diego Business Journal, San Diego Magazine, and San Diego Union-Tribune Business.

- **Conferences and Trade Shows:** Attend conferences and trade shows relevant to your industry, such as the San Diego Startup Week, San Diego Innovation Summit, and San Diego Small Business Expo, to network with industry professionals and gain insights into emerging trends.

- **Business Networking Organizations:** Join business networking organizations in San Diego, such as the San Diego Regional Chamber of Commerce, San Diego Entrepreneurs Exchange, and San Diego Business Networking Group, to connect with local entrepreneurs, share experiences, and explore collaborative opportunities.

- **Local Meetups and Events:** Participate in local meetups and events through platforms like Meetup.com and Eventbrite, where you

can meet fellow entrepreneurs, exchange ideas, and stay informed about the latest happenings in San Diego's business community.

- **Industry Forums and Online Communities:** Engage in online industry forums and communities specific to your field to connect with professionals, share knowledge, and stay updated on industry trends.
- **Market Research Reports:** Access market research reports specific to San Diego or your industry to gain insights into consumer behavior, market trends, and competitive analysis.

- **Professional Networking Platforms:** Utilize professional networking platforms like LinkedIn to expand your professional network, connect with industry influencers, and stay connected with the San Diego business community.
- **Industry Reports:** Access industry reports from market research companies like IBISWorld, Statista, Vertical IQ, or MarketResearch.com to gain insights into the market size, growth rates, and key industry trends.
- **News and Publications:** Follow industry-specific publications, online blogs, and news outlets to stay updated on the latest happenings, emerging technologies, and shifts in consumer behavior.

Explore Customer Preferences:

Understanding what makes your target audience tick is essential for crafting offerings that resonate with their desires. Uncover their needs, wants, and pain points through customer surveys, focus groups, and one-on-one interviews. Know their preferences, motivations, and buying behaviors to tailor your products or services accordingly. Meeting customer expectations is the ultimate way to ride the wave of success.

- **Customer Surveys and Feedback:** In addition to online surveys, tools like Typeform or Qualtrics can help you create engaging and interactive surveys to collect feedback and understand customer preferences.
- **Social Media Listening:** Leverage social media monitoring tools like Mention to track conversations and sentiment about your brand or industry. This helps you understand customer sentiment and identify emerging trends.

Sample Table 1: Customer Survey Results

Question	Strongly Agree	Agree	Neutral	Disagree	Strongly Disagree
Product quality	45%	35%	15%	3%	2%
Pricing	20%	40%	25%	10%	5%
Customer service	30%	40%	20%	5%	5%
Brand reputation	25%	30%	30%	10%	5%

Study Your Competitors Like a Pro:

Surfing wouldn't be half as exciting without friendly competition, and the same goes for the business world. You need to study your competitors to stay ahead of the game. Analyze their strengths and weaknesses, observe their marketing strategies, and identify any gaps or opportunities you can leverage. By understanding the competitive landscape, you can position your business uniquely and ride the wave of differentiation.

- **Competitor Analysis Tools:** Tools like SEMrush, SpyFu, or SimilarWeb provide insights into your competitors' online presence, keywords, advertising strategies, and traffic sources.

- **Social Media Analysis:** Analyze your competitors' social media presence, engagement, and content strategies using tools like Sprout Social, Hootsuite Insights, or Brandwatch.

Sample Table 2: Competitive Analysis

Competitor	Strengths	Weaknesses	Opportunities	Threats
Competitor 1	Strong brand recognition	High pricing	Growing market segment	New entrants
Competitor 2	Quality products	Limited distribution	Increasing consumer demand	Shifting consumer preferences
Competitor 3	Competitive pricing	Lack of innovation	Expanding into new markets	Economic downturn

Riding the Waves of Demand:

Armed with a deep understanding of the San Diego market, it's time to deliver products and services that truly resonate with the local community. You'll be able to identify the sweet spots in the market where your offerings will make the biggest splash. Stay flexible, adapt to changing tides, and continuously fine-tune your strategies based on the insights you gather from your market research endeavors.

Developing a Business Plan:

Every successful business needs a well-crafted business plan as sturdy as the iconic Hotel del Coronado. Taking charge of the process, you must develop a comprehensive plan outlining your success roadmap. From the executive summary that captures the essence of your business to the financial projections that keep your ship afloat, it is your responsibility to cover it all. Check out Appendix A for a sample business plan template.

Resources:
• Resources for Creating a Business Model Canvas and Business Plan: To create a business model canvas, you can utilize online tools such as Canvanizer (https://canvanizer.com/) or Strategyzer's Business Model Canvas (https://www.strategyzer.com/). These platforms offer user-friendly templates to help you shape your business model like a master sand sculptor.
• When it comes to developing a comprehensive business plan, you can refer to resources such as the Small Business Administration's (SBA) Business Plan Template (https://www.sba.gov/business-guide/plan-your-business/write-your-business-plan) or Bplans' Sample Business Plans (https://www.bplans.com/sample_business_plans.php). These resources are intended to guide you through the process, ensuring your business plan is as solid as a well-built sandcastle.

Case Study: A Day in the Life of "TacoTide" - A San Diego Food Truck

Step 1:   **Defining the Business Idea:** The founders of TacoTide, a San Diego food truck, had a passion for Mexican cuisine and a vision to bring delicious tacos to local beachgoers.

Step 2:   **Conducting Market Research:** They researched the local food truck industry, analyzed customer preferences, and scouted potential locations near popular beaches.

Step 3:   **Developing a Business Plan:** The founders crafted a business plan that outlined their concept, target market, marketing strategies, financial projections, and necessary permits and licenses.

Step 4:   **Registering the Business:** TacoTide registered its business name, obtained a Federal Employer Identification Number (EIN), and applied for the required state and local permits to operate a food truck.

Step 5:   **Building the Brand:** They created a unique brand identity for TacoTide, designing a catchy logo, developing a mouthwatering menu, and establishing an active presence on social media platforms.

Step 6:   **Launching and Marketing:** TacoTide hit the streets of San Diego, making appearances at local beach events, partnering with nearby businesses, and leveraging social media to generate buzz and attract customers.

Step 7:   **Continuous Improvement:** The founders collected customer feedback, adjusted their menu based on preferences, optimized their operations for efficiency, and refined their marketing strategies to stay competitive.

Step 8:   **Expanding and Diversifying:** After establishing a loyal customer base, TacoTide expanded its offerings by introducing new taco varieties, partnering with local suppliers for fresh ingredients, and exploring catering opportunities.

Through their dedication and strategic planning, TacoTide carved a niche for itself in the San Diego food scene, becoming a beloved beachside culinary delight.

As you embark on your own entrepreneurial journey, don't forget that planning and research are not merely stepping stones to success but integral parts of the adventure itself. Embrace the process, learn from the insights you gather, and let the spirit of San Diego's entrepreneurial community guide you toward a future filled with joy, triumph, and lasting memories.

Conclusion:

In this chapter, we explored the crucial steps of planning and research for your small business bliss. By defining your business idea, conducting thorough market research, and developing a comprehensive business plan, you'll set sail on a path to success. Like the diverse neighborhoods of San Diego, every small business has its unique charm and opportunities. So let your entrepreneurial spirit shine as you embark on this exciting adventure!

And now, a joke: Why did the scarecrow become a successful entrepreneur?

Because he was outstanding in his field!

Chapter 2: Legal Considerations

Welcome to Chapter 2, my fellow adventurers in the entrepreneurial realm, where we dive headfirst into the intriguing world of legal considerations. Now, before you start conjuring images of stuffy lawyers and mountains of paperwork, let me assure you that we're about to hop on a thrilling ride filled with unexpected twists and turns.

Now, you might be thinking, "Papers? We don't need no stinking paper!" But hold on, my entrepreneurial friend, because understanding and complying with legal considerations is crucial to the success and longevity of any business endeavor.

Let me share an interesting caper, as one of my business ventures gained momentum and I found myself in the exhilarating world of venture capital raises, legal considerations took on a whole new level of complexity. Meetings with legal advisors became a regular occurrence, as we navigated the intricacies of contracts, intellectual property protection, and regulatory compliance. It was like engaging in a high-stakes poker game, where understanding the rules and having a strong legal hand was essential to securing investment and protecting our interests.

This story underscores the importance of understanding legal requirements. During my quest to start a nonprofit organization, I learned firsthand the arduous path one must tread to obtain that coveted 501(c)(3) status. It involved countless hours poring over legal documents, submitting meticulously prepared applications, and engaging in dialogue with legal advisors who were like guides in this unfamiliar territory.

Ah, but let's not forget the growing challenges of managing a workforce. As our team expanded, so did the complexities of human resources. Employment laws, benefits, and the ever-evolving landscape of labor regulations kept us on our toes. In our quest to manage HR challenges effectively, we discovered the power of outsourcing risk, tapping into the expertise of HR professionals who could navigate the legal nuances and keep us compliant while we focused on our core business.

Remember, while legal considerations may seem daunting, they are the guardians of our business ventures, protecting us from potential pitfalls and ensuring a solid foundation for growth. So, let's venture forth together, armed with knowledge, and the determination to conquer the legal landscape, one legal document at a time.

Legal Considerations: Breaking the Chains of Risk and Red Tape:

Welcome to the legal side of small business in sunny San Diego! As you launch your entrepreneurial life, it's essential to navigate the legal landscape with confidence and clarity. In this chapter, explore the key legal considerations that can impact your small business's success. From choosing the right business structure to complying with labor laws and utilizing free legal assistance, it's important to take responsibility for researching, learning, and understanding this information as you establish your business in San Diego.

Choosing the Right Business Structure:

Just like the diverse neighborhoods of San Diego, there are different business structures to choose from, each with its advantages and legal implications. It's crucial for you to understand the options, including sole proprietorship, partnership, limited liability company (LLC), and corporation Selecting the right structure for your business can establish a solid legal foundation to support your entrepreneurial endeavors.

Registering Your Business:

Before you can begin your small business adventure, you will need to go through the registration process, much like getting a ticket to a Padres game at Petco Park. It's your responsibility to navigate the steps of registering your business, including business name registration, obtaining a Federal Employer Identification Number (EIN), and applying for state and local licenses and permits. With the right registrations in place, you'll be ready to launch your business with confidence.

Understanding Intellectual Property:

In the creative and innovative city of San Diego, the responsibility falls on you to protect your intellectual property. You should seek professional support to delve into the world of trademarks, copyrights, and patents, understanding the significance of safeguarding your unique ideas, brand names, logos, and inventions. Just as the iconic Balboa Park preserves the city's cultural heritage, protecting your intellectual property ensures the preservation of your business's distinct identity.

Intellectual property (IP) encompasses creations of the mind, such as inventions, designs, brand names, and artistic works. To gain a deeper understanding of IP, entrepreneurs can refer to resources provided by the United States Patent and Trademark Office (www.uspto.gov) and the World Intellectual Property Organization (www.wipo.int). These organizations offer comprehensive guides, tutorials, and databases to help individuals navigate the intricacies of patents, trademarks, copyrights, and trade secrets.

Managing Licenses and Permits:

Operating a small business in San Diego demands compliance with specific licenses and permits. You will need to gain an understanding of the licenses and permits that may be required, including those regulated at the local, state, and federal levels. From health permits for food establishments to zoning permits for physical locations, you need to navigate the necessary paperwork and ensure compliance to keep your business running smoothly.

The City of San Diego's official website offers a comprehensive guide to business licensing, including information on the specific permits required for different types of businesses. Entrepreneurs can access the San Diego Business Portal (business.sandiego.gov) to learn about zoning regulations, health and safety permits, environmental permits, and other compliance requirements.

Furthermore, national-level resources such as the Small Business Administration (SBA) and the Business.USA.gov website provide entrepreneurs with valuable information and tools to understand licensing and permit obligations across various industries and states. These resources can guide business owners through the process of obtaining the necessary permits, ensuring legal compliance, and avoiding potential penalties or setbacks.

Complying with Labor Laws:
Like the fair and inclusive spirit of San Diego, your small business must comply with labor laws to foster a harmonious and productive work environment.

Let's delve into employment regulations, workplace safety, and health standards, fair labor standards, and anti-discrimination laws. By researching, learning, and understanding these laws, you will create a supportive and compliant workplace for your employees.

The U.S. Department of Labor (DOL) serves as a valuable resource for understanding and complying with labor laws. The DOL's website (www.dol.gov) provides detailed information on topics such as minimum wage, overtime pay, workplace safety, anti-discrimination laws, and employee benefits. Entrepreneurs can access educational materials, guidelines, and compliance assistance to ensure their business meets labor law requirements.

In addition to federal regulations, the state of California has specific labor laws that entrepreneurs must understand and follow. The California Department of Industrial Relations (DIR) offers comprehensive resources to help business owners navigate labor laws in the state. Entrepreneurs can visit the DIR website (www.dir.ca.gov) for information on wage and hour regulations, workplace safety standards, employee rights, and compliance tools.

Use the resources below and take proactive steps to protect your intellectual property, comply with labor laws, and utilize available legal resources, you will strengthen your business's foundation and position it for long-term success.

Resources:
• Applying for an Employer Identification Number (EIN) https://www.irs.gov/businesses/small-businesses-self-employed/apply-for-an-employer-identification-number-ein-online
• Small Business Administration (SBA) Guide to Choosing Your Business Structure: SBA Guide - https://www.sba.gov/business-guide/launch-your-business/choose-business-structure
• San Diego County Business Registration: San Diego Business Registration - https://www.sandiegocounty.gov/content/sdc/ttc/services/regbusinesses.html

• U.S. Patent and Trademark Office: USPTO - https://www.uspto.gov/
• California Department of Industrial Relations: California Labor Law Resources - https://www.dir.ca.gov/
• San Diego Volunteer Lawyer Program: SDVLP - https://sdvlp.org/
• Thomas Jefferson School of Law Clinic: TJSL Clinic - https://www.tjsl.edu/clinics
• USD Law Clinic: USD Law Clinic - https://www.sandiego.edu/law/
• Legal Aid Society: Legal Aid Society - https://www.lassd.org/

Case Study: Brewtopia - Crafting Success in San Diego

Brewtopia, a small craft brewery located in the heart of San Diego, serves as a prime example of successfully navigating the legal considerations in the city. Let's take a look at how Brewtopia approached the legal aspects of its business:

Step 1:   **Choosing the Right Business Structure:** Brewtopia evaluated its business goals, liability concerns, and growth potential and decided to establish a limited liability company (LLC) structure to protect its personal assets while allowing flexibility for growth.

Step 2:   **Registering the Business:** Brewtopia registered its business name with the San Diego County Clerk's Office and obtained an EIN from the IRS.

Step 3:   **Protecting Intellectual Property:** Brewtopia trademarked its unique logo and brand name to distinguish itself in the competitive craft beer market.

Step 4:   **Managing Licenses and Permits:**
Brewtopia obtained necessary permits from
the California Department of Alcoholic
Beverage Control, the San Diego Health
Department, and the city's zoning
department.

Step 5:   **Complying with Labor Laws:**
Brewtopia adhered to fair labor standards,
provided a safe working environment, and
implemented anti-discrimination policies to
foster a positive workplace culture.

Step 6:   **Utilizing Legal Assistance:** When
facing trademark infringement issues,
Brewtopia sought guidance from the San
Diego Volunteer Lawyer Program, receiving
pro bono legal assistance to protect its
intellectual property rights.

Conclusion:
In this chapter, we explored the legal considerations
of starting and running a small business in San

Diego. By choosing the right business structure, registering your business, protecting your intellectual property, managing licenses and permits, complying with labor laws, and utilizing free legal assistance, you'll build a strong legal foundation for your entrepreneurial venture. Remember, legal compliance is key to thriving in the sun-soaked business landscape of San Diego.

**Note: Please be aware that the mentioned resources are for reference purposes, and it's advisable to consult legal professionals for specific legal advice tailored to your business.

And now, let's conclude with a legal-themed joke to bring a smile to your face:

Why did the business owner bring a ruler to the licensing office?

Because they wanted to measure up to all the legal requirements!

Chapter 3: Building a Strong Brand

Understanding your customers' pain points is like
possessing a hidden key that unlocks the door to
their hearts and minds. It empowers you to tailor your

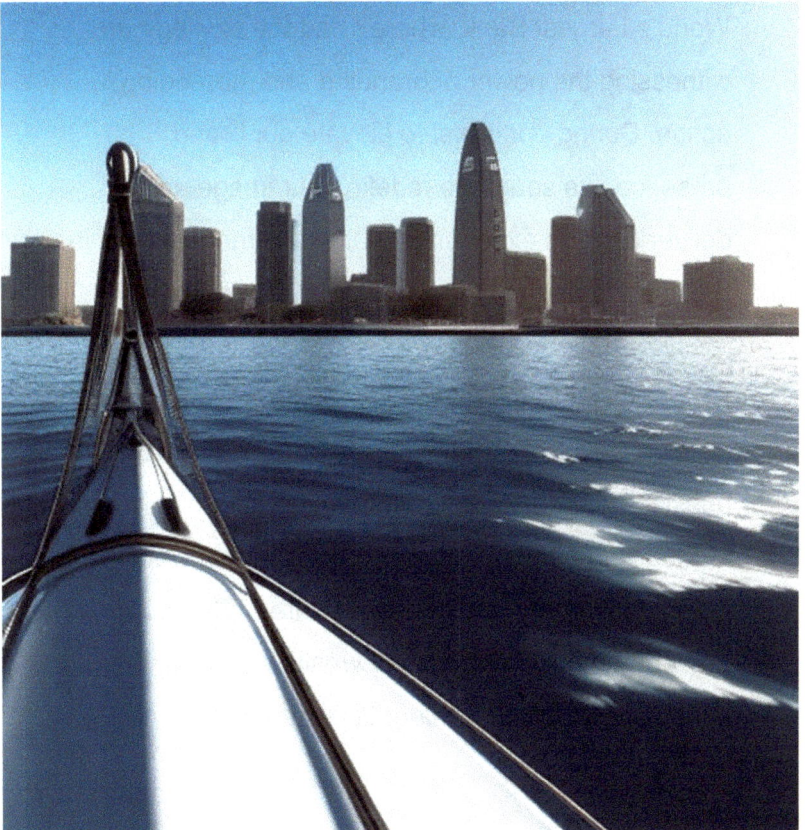

products, services, and brand messaging to effectively address their needs, desires, and aspirations. You will need to delve into the psyche of your target audience, gathering clues and piecing together a brand strategy that will leave them exclaiming, "Wow, they truly understand me!"

Allow me to share a personal tale from my time at the World's Largest Bank, where I had the privilege of witnessing the power of branding and rebranding in action. During our quest to elevate our brand presence, we sought to redefine our image and deliver a brand experience that would make waves in the financial industry.

Picture this: I found myself in a bustling conference room in New York City, surrounded by a team of passionate marketers, brainstorming, and strategizing as we customized a brand that would reflect the vibrant and diverse culture of San Diego. We wanted our pre-launch of wealth management centers to resonate with our target audience and convey our commitment to understanding their unique needs.

We dug deep into our brand persona, unraveling the essence of who we were and what we stood for. We crafted a value proposition that would become our guiding light, ensuring that every touchpoint with our clients reflected our commitment to delivering exceptional value and unparalleled service. It was like sculpting a work of art, carefully shaping our brand identity to align with the aspirations and values of our clients.

As we unveiled our reimagined brand, the response was electrifying. We witnessed firsthand the power of a strong brand in forging connections, building trust, and ultimately driving business success. Our brand became a symbol of reliability, expertise, and a commitment to transforming our clients' financial success.

So, my fellow brand builders, in this chapter, we'll delve into the intricacies of building a strong brand that not only captures attention but also captures hearts. We'll explore the elements of brand identity, the importance of understanding your target audience, and the art of crafting a compelling value proposition that sets you apart from the competition.

Remember, building a strong brand is not a one-time endeavor—it's a continuous cycle of self-reflection, adaptation, and innovation. So, let's embrace our inner brand warriors, armed with creativity, market insights, and a touch of whimsy, as we navigate the exhilarating world of brand building.

Building a Strong Brand: Painting Success, One Brushstroke at a Time

Welcome to the world of brand building, where creativity meets strategy and storytelling takes center stage. In this chapter, you will enter the process of creating a strong brand that resonates with your target audience and sets your small business apart from the competition. So, let's embark on this branding endeavor together and unlock the secrets to building a remarkable brand.

Defining Your Brand Identity:

Like the waves of the Pacific Ocean that define San Diego's coastal charm, your brand identity sets the tone for your business. You will need to explore how to define your brand's mission, values, personality, and unique selling propositions. Understanding the core elements of your brand will lay a solid foundation for creating an identity that connects with your target audience.

Creating an Effective Brand Strategy:
In the bustling business scene of San Diego, a well-crafted brand strategy is essential. You will need to identify the process of defining your target market, conducting competitive analysis, and positioning your brand in the marketplace. By developing a comprehensive brand strategy, you'll have a roadmap that aligns your business goals with your brand's identity and connects with your ideal customers.

Designing a Memorable Logo and Visual Identity:
Your logo and visual identity are the face of your brand, just like the iconic Hotel del Coronado represents the beauty and elegance of San Diego. You will need to explore the principles of effective logo design and visual branding, including color theory, typography, and imagery. With the right visual

elements, you'll create a memorable brand identity that leaves a lasting impression on your audience.

Remember, it is up to you to research, learn, and understand this information as you delve into the world of brand building. By taking ownership of the process, you'll have the knowledge and tools to create a brand that stands out in the competitive landscape. So, get ready to unleash your creativity and build a remarkable brand for your small business.

Crafting a Compelling Brand Story:
San Diego is a city of stories, from its historic landmarks to its vibrant cultural heritage. Your brand needs a compelling story that captivates and engages your audience. Show you crafted a brand story that communicates your brand's values, resonates with your target audience, and sets you apart from competitors. With the unique design of your narrative, you'll forge a deeper connection with your customers and foster brand loyalty.

Developing a Consistent Brand Voice:

Just as the diverse communities of San Diego celebrate their distinct voices, your brand needs a consistent voice that reflects its personality and values. In this chapter, you'll delve into the importance of defining your brand's tone, language, and messaging guidelines. With the maintenance of a consistent brand voice across all communication channels, you'll build trust, establish credibility, and create a cohesive brand experience for your customers.

Resources:
• Brand Identity Guide: For a comprehensive guide on defining your brand identity, check out this resource: Brand Identity Guide - https://brandpacks.com/best-brand-guidelines-manual-templates-indesign/
• Logo Design Inspiration: Find inspiration for your logo design from various sources, including websites like Behance and Dribbble. Browse through their galleries of well-designed logos to spark your creativity.
• Color Palette Generators: Use online color-palette generators such as Coolors and Adobe Color to create harmonious color schemes. Experiment with different

combinations to find the perfect colors that represent your brand's personality.
• Typography Resources: Explore typography resources like Google Fonts and Font Squirrel to discover a wide range of fonts and learn about effective typography techniques. Select fonts that complement your brand identity and enhance the readability of your brand materials.
• Storytelling Techniques: Learn effective storytelling techniques from resources like Pixar's 22 Rules of Storytelling and Storytelling for Business. These resources provide valuable insights and tips to help you craft compelling brand stories.
• Writing Style Guides: Establish consistent writing guidelines with the help of style guides like The Chicago Manual of Style and AP Stylebook. These guides offer rules and best practices for creating a cohesive brand voice in your written communications.

Case Study: Breezy Bites - A Flavorful Brand in San Diego

Breezy Bites, a San Diego-based food truck specializing in gourmet tacos, began a branding plan that captures the essence of their business. These are the sequential steps they took to build their brand:

Step 1:   **Brand Identity:** Breezy Bites defined its brand identity by focusing on its mission to provide fresh, innovative flavors with a laid-back beach vibe. They identified their target audience as local food enthusiasts and tourists looking for a

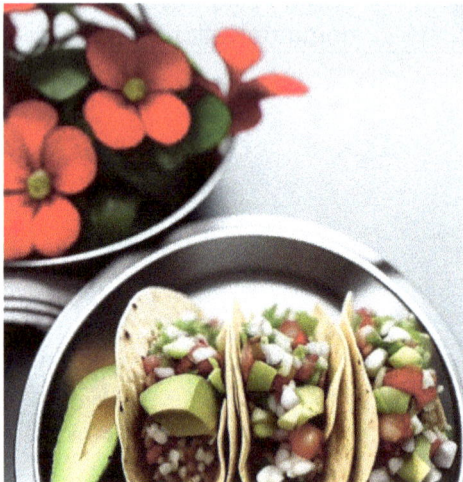

unique culinary experience in San Diego.

Step 2:   **Brand Strategy:** They conducted market research, analyzed competitors, and positioned itself as the go-to food truck for gourmet taco lovers. They crafted a brand strategy that highlighted their fresh ingredients, bold flavors, and commitment to sustainability, aligning their brand with the eco-conscious values of San Diego residents.

Step 3:   **Visual Identity:** They collaborated with a local designer to create a logo that incorporated elements of ocean waves and vibrant colors reminiscent of San Diego's coastal scenery. They developed a visual identity that

exuded a sense of fun, freshness, and
culinary creativity.

Step 4:   **Brand Story:** They crafted a brand
story that celebrated their passion for tacos,
local ingredients, and the joy of sharing
flavorful meals with friends and family. They
shared their story of becoming a beloved
fixture in San Diego's food scene.

Step 5:   **Brand Voice:** Breezy Bites adopted a
friendly, casual, and approachable brand
voice that mirrored the laid-back culture of
San Diego. They used social media, their
website, and in-person interactions to
communicate their brand's personality and
connect with their audience.

Conclusion:
In this chapter, we delved into the art of building a
strong brand that captures the essence of your
business and connects with your target audience.
Understanding the importance of brand identity and

formulating a strategic brand strategy can lay the foundation for a remarkable brand presence. Crafting a compelling brand story and adopting a consistent brand voice further enhance your brand's authenticity and resonance. Just like the warm San Diego sun, a strong brand leaves a lasting impression and sets the stage for your business's success.

And now, for a light-hearted joke: Why don't scientists trust atoms?

Because they make up everything!

Chapter 4: Developing Your Products or Services

Welcome, dear readers, to Chapter 4, where we discover how to create remarkable products and services that captivate our customers' hearts and bring prosperity to our business. As we enter into the exciting path of product development, let's remember that even though we may not always get exactly what we want, we can strive to create offerings that exceed expectations and leave a lasting impact.

In this chapter, we'll explore the art of developing products and services that meet the needs of our target audience while ensuring a healthy balance between cost, quality, and profitability. But fret not, my friends, for we shall navigate this terrain with a lighthearted touch, embracing the joy and creativity that comes with crafting remarkable offerings.

Understanding the key metrics of business success is like wielding a compass that guides us on the path to prosperity. We'll delve into the intricacies of knowing our cost of acquisition, cost of goods and services, and profit margins. Armed with this knowledge, we can make informed decisions that not only drive revenue but also foster sustainable growth.

Allow me to share a tale from my time at Precision Information, a dynamic learning management software company, where I had the pleasure of leading a strategic change in product development. Picture this: a vibrant workspace filled with agile minds, where product designers and marketers converged to create something truly exceptional.

We engaged on a mission to understand our clients' needs, to grasp the intricate dance between their desires and our capabilities. We employed a strategic design approach, considering the four Ps: product, price, placement, and prosperity of people. Each element played a crucial role in our quest to deliver unparalleled value and forge lasting connections with our customers.

Gathered around a whiteboard adorned with colorful sketches and mind maps, our lean product and marketing teams sparked a synergy that fueled our creative process. We ventured into the depths of user research, market analysis, and prototyping, striving to transform insights into scalable and innovative offerings.

We sought to grasp not only what our customers wanted but also what they truly needed. We understood that success lay in going beyond surface-level desires and addressing their underlying pain points. As we embraced empathy and a deep understanding of our clients' challenges, we crafted products and services that offered solutions with a touch of enchantment.

So, my fellow product pioneers, in this chapter, we'll step forward on a thrilling expedition into the world of product development. Discover the importance of market research, customer feedback, and strategic pricing. Understand the magic of turning ideas into tangible offerings that leave a lasting impression and contribute to our customers' success.

In the real business world, developing remarkable products and services is an ongoing endeavor—one that requires adaptability, curiosity, and a sprinkle of audacity. Let's unleash our creativity, embrace the unexpected, and strive to delight our customers with offerings that exceed their wildest dreams.

Business Growth Strategies: Scaling New Heights in the Marketplace:

Welcome to the exciting space of product and service development, where innovation and customer needs converge. In this chapter, you will need to explore the crucial steps involved in bringing your products or services to life. Innovative startups that thrive in San Diego's dynamic business landscape navigate through the process of identifying their target markets, conducting research and development, implementing pricing strategies, prototyping and testing, and creating comprehensive launch plans. So, let's transform your ideas into tangible offerings that meet customer demands and drive business success.

Identifying Your Target Market:
Just as the diverse

neighborhoods of San Diego cater to different interests, understanding your target market is essential for product or service development. You will need to identify your ideal customers by considering demographics, psychographics, and market segmentation. By understanding your target market's preferences, pain points, and desires, you'll be better equipped to develop products or services that truly resonate with them.

Conducting Product or Service Research and Development:
Innovation is at the heart of successful businesses, and thorough research and development lay the

groundwork for breakthrough products or services. Take time to explore different research methods, such as surveys, focus groups, and market analysis, to gather insights about customer needs, industry trends, and competitors. Know that by leveraging this knowledge, you can refine your offerings and create unique value propositions that set your business apart.

Pricing Strategies and Profit Margins:
Determining the right pricing strategy is a delicate balancing act, much like capturing the perfect sunset view from the shores of San Diego. In this chapter, you will need to delve into various pricing models, such as cost-plus pricing, value-based pricing, and competitive pricing, to help you set optimal price points for your products or services. It will be up to you to explore and understand how to strike a balance between profitability and competitiveness in your pricing strategy while considering profit margins.

Understanding Customer Perceptions:

Price is more than just a number; it holds significant value in the eyes of your customers. In this section, we shed light on the importance of understanding customer perceptions when it comes to pricing. Learn how to conduct market research, surveys, and customer interviews to gauge the perceived value of your products or services. Understanding your target audience's willingness to pay, their price sensitivity, and their expectations, can help align your pricing strategy with their needs and position your business for success.

Prototyping and Testing:

Like the iterative process of perfecting a craft beer recipe, prototyping and testing are crucial for refining your products or services. You will need to navigate the steps of creating prototypes and conducting thorough testing to ensure your offerings meet quality standards and customer expectations. By embracing a culture of continuous improvement, you can fine-tune your products or services to deliver exceptional value. Don't forget, the responsibility lies with you to research and learn the best practices for prototyping and testing.

Creating a Product or Service Launch Plan:
Launching your products or services with a bang requires careful planning and execution. In this chapter, you will need to understand the essential elements of a product or service launch plan. This includes setting launch objectives, identifying target audiences, designing marketing strategies, and coordinating logistics. In crafting a comprehensive launch plan, you can create excitement, generate buzz, and maximize the impact of your offerings in the market. It will be your responsibility to research, learn, and apply the strategies that align with your specific business goals.

Here are several key steps:

Step 1:   **Define Launch Objectives:** Set clear and measurable goals for your launch, such as sales targets or brand awareness.

Step 2:   **Conduct Market Research:** Understand your target audience, competitors, and market trends through thorough research.

Step 3:   **Develop a Unique Value Proposition:** Craft a compelling value proposition that sets your offering apart from the competition.

Step 4:   **Design Marketing Strategies:** Create a comprehensive marketing plan using various channels and tactics to generate buzz.

Step 5:   **Coordinate Logistics:** Ensure all necessary logistics, such as inventory, production, and customer support, are in place.

Step 6:   **Execute the Launch:** Implement your plan with precision, engaging your audience through captivating campaigns.

Embrace the challenges and opportunities that come your way, and may your path be paved with success and growth.

Resources:
• Market Research Tools: Utilize market research tools such as "SurveyMonkey" and "Google Trends" to gather valuable insights about your target market, industry trends, and competitor analysis.
• Pricing Strategy Guides: Learn about effective pricing strategies from resources like "HubSpot's Pricing Strategy Guide" and "Neil Patel's Pricing Strategy 101." These guides offer practical tips and techniques for determining optimal pricing for your products or services.
• Prototyping and Testing Resources: Explore prototyping and testing resources like "InVision" and "UserTesting" to gain insights into best practices, tools, and methodologies refining your offerings.
• Launch Planning Templates: Streamline your product or service launch planning with ready-to-use templates like "Trello's Launch Plan Template" and "Asana's Product Launch Checklist." These templates provide a framework for organizing and executing a successful launch.

Case Study - OceanFit:

OceanFit is a small business based in San Diego that specializes in swimwear for active beachgoers and fitness enthusiasts. Here are the sequential steps

taken by OceanFit in developing its swimwear
products:

Step 1:   **Identifying the Target Market:**
OceanFit conducted market research and
identified its target market as active
individuals who value performance and
sustainability in swimwear.

Step 2:   **Research and Development:** The
team at OceanFit conducted extensive
research on sustainable materials and
innovative design techniques to create
swimwear that meets their target market's
needs and preferences.

Step 3:   **Pricing Strategies and Profit
Margins:** OceanFit employed a value-based
pricing strategy, positioning their swimwear as
high-quality performance gear. They carefully
calculated their profit margins to ensure
sustainability and competitiveness in the
market.

Step 4:

Prototyping and Testing: OceanFit created multiple prototypes of their swimwear designs and conducted rigorous testing to ensure optimal fit, comfort, and durability. They incorporated feedback from focus groups and made iterative improvements to their products.

Step 5: **Product Launch Plan:** OceanFit developed a comprehensive launch plan that included social media marketing, collaborations with local fitness influencers, and participation in beach events and expos. They created anticipation and excitement

around their swimwear brand, leading to a successful launch.

Conclusion:

Developing outstanding products or services requires a deep understanding of your target market, diligent research and development, strategic pricing, meticulous prototyping and testing, and a well-executed launch plan. The sequential steps outlined in this chapter will set you on your way to creating offerings that resonate with customers and drive business success. Embrace the spirit of innovation found in San Diego, and let your products or services make a splash in the market.

And now, for a joke:

Why did the math book look sad?

Because it had too many problems! Let's make sure our products and services are the solution to our customers' problems, bringing them joy and prosperity.

Chapter 5: Sales and Marketing Strategies

Welcome, my fellow sales and marketing enthusiasts. Get ready to immerse into the exhilarating world of sales and marketing strategies, where creativity meets analytics and where the power of persuasion takes center stage. But hold on tight, because, in this chapter, we're about to shake things up and break free from traditional marketing clichés!

When it comes to marketing, it's not simply a matter of canning eggs to place them on top of the shopping bag. Oh no, dear friends, marketing is a vibrant dance that harmonizes creativity and analysis, a delightful symphony of strategies crafted to captivate the hearts and minds of our target audience.

In this chapter, we will delve into the art of creating and tracking conversion rates across multiple campaigns. The objective is to uncover the secrets that unlock the true potential of your marketing efforts and maximize your return on investment. From brainstorming captivating campaigns to measuring their impact, the onus will be on you to leave no stone unturned.

So, gear up and get ready to be empowered with the knowledge and skills to take your marketing endeavors to new heights. It is through your own research, learning, and understanding that you will gain mastery in this dynamic field. Let's discover the wonders that await us in the arena of marketing strategy and analysis.

Allow me to share another personal tale from my time at Precision Information, the cutting-edge learning management software company. Picture this: we were on the brink of launching a revolutionary new product, poised to take the market by storm. We knew that a successful launch required more than just a flashy website and a catchy tagline.

Together with our talented marketing teams, we planned to design promotional campaigns that would resonate with our target audience. We delved deep into understanding their needs, their pain points, and their aspirations. Armed with this knowledge, we crafted captivating messages that spoke directly to their hearts and minds.

We knew that tracking and measuring the success of our campaigns was paramount. We became Master of Data analysis, using key metrics and conversion rates to fine-tune our strategies and optimize our marketing efforts. We were like detectives, sleuthing our way through the marketing landscape, always on the hunt for new insights and innovative approaches. Let's stroll into the world of sales and marketing strategies with a fresh perspective. Discover how to create campaigns that leave a lasting impression, connect with our audience on a deeper level, and ultimately deliver on our value proposition.

Marketing is an ever-evolving adventure, and in this chapter, we're about to embark on a thrilling ride. So, fasten your seatbelts and get ready to revolutionize your approach to sales and marketing. It's time to think differently, act boldly, and watch your business soar to new heights!

Sales and Marketing Strategies: Sealing the Deal and Making it Rain:

In this chapter, you will explore various sales and marketing strategies that will help you reach your target audience, build brand awareness, and cultivate strong customer relationships. From traditional advertising and promotion to the power of social media, search engine optimization, public relations, and customer relationship management, these tools are necessary to develop a robust sales and marketing strategy that aligns with your business goals.

Traditional Advertising and Promotion:

In a world where digital marketing dominates, traditional advertising and promotion methods still hold their ground. Define your goals and determine the impact of traditional channels such as print media, radio, television, and outdoor advertising. Understanding how to craft compelling messages and leverage these platforms will enable you to effectively reach your target audience in the vibrant city of San Diego.

Table 1: Traditional Advertising Platforms

Platform	Description	Typical Goals
Print Media	Newspapers, magazines, brochures, flyers, etc.	Increase brand visibility, reach local audience
Radio	Broadcasting commercials or sponsored segments on radio stations	Drive awareness, target specific demographics
Television	Air television commercials or sponsor TV programs	Broad reach, showcase visual content
Outdoor Advertising	Billboards, signage, bus shelters, etc.	Increase local visibility, generate curiosity

Social Media and Content Marketing:

In the age of social media, establishing a strong online presence is essential. Your business will need to cultivate social media and content marketing, exploring popular platforms like Facebook, Instagram, Twitter, and LinkedIn. By researching and learning strategies for creating engaging content, building a loyal following, and leveraging user-generated content, you can amplify your brand's reach and make a meaningful impact.

Table 2: Social Media Platforms

Platform	Description	Typical Goals
Facebook	Largest social media platform with diverse targeting options	Build brand awareness, engage with customers
Instagram	Visual-focused platform for sharing photos and videos	Showcase products, inspire, and engage a younger audience
Twitter	Microblogging platform with short messages (tweets)	Drive real-time engagement, share updates and announcements
LinkedIn	Professional networking platform	B2B marketing, establish industry authority

Search Engine Optimization (SEO) and Online Advertising:

With so many businesses vying for attention online, understanding search engine optimization (SEO) and online advertising is crucial. Unravel the mysteries of SEO and research actionable tips to improve your website's visibility in search engine results. Additionally, exploring online advertising platforms such as Google Ads and social media advertising will enable you to target specific audiences and maximize your marketing return on investment (ROI).

Table 3: Online Advertising Platforms

Platform	Description	Typical Goals
Google Ads	Pay-per-click advertising platform on Google search engine and partner websites	Drive website traffic, increase conversions
Facebook Ads	Targeted advertising on Facebook and Instagram based on user demographics and interests	Reach specific audience segments, generate leads
LinkedIn Ads	Advertising on LinkedIn targeting professionals based on job titles, industries, etc.	B2B marketing, network with industry professionals

Public Relations and Media Outreach:

Building a positive brand image and gaining media exposure can significantly impact your business's growth. You will need to delve into the world of public relations (PR) and media outreach, researching strategies to develop relationships with journalists, pitch compelling stories, and secure media coverage. By harnessing the power of PR, you can generate buzz, enhance credibility, and expand your reach.

Table 4: PR and Media Outreach Strategies

Strategy	Description	Typical Goals
Press Releases	Official statements sent to media outlets announcing newsworthy events, products, or updates	Gain media coverage, enhance brand reputation
Media Pitches	Personalized pitches sent to journalists and media personnel to secure coverage or interviews	Generate media interest, establish thought leadership
Influencer Collaborations	Partnering with influencers to promote products or services through their social media channels	Reach a wider audience, leverage influencers' credibility, and reach

Customer Relationship Management (CRM):
Nurturing strong relationships with your customers is key to long-term success. Explore the concept of customer relationship management (CRM) and how it can help you provide personalized experiences, build

customer loyalty, and drive repeat business. Researching and learning about implementing CRM software, utilizing email marketing, and implementing loyalty programs will equip you with strategies to strengthen your bond with customers.

Table 5: CRM Metrics

Metric	Description	Typical Goals
Customer Churn Rate	Percentage of customers who stop using or purchasing from your business within a specific time period	Reduce customer churn, improve customer retention
Customer Satisfaction Score (CSAT)	Measure of customer satisfaction based on surveys or feedback	Improve customer experience and loyalty
Net Promoter Score (NPS)	Indicator of customer loyalty and likelihood to recommend the business	Identify promoters and detractors, measure brand advocacy

1. **Customer Churn Rate:** Customer Churn Rate is calculated by dividing the number of customers who churned during a specific period by the total number of customers at the beginning of that period.

Formula: Churn Rate = (Customers Churned / Total Customers) * 100

2. **Customer Satisfaction Score (CSAT):**
   Customer Satisfaction Score is typically obtained through surveys or feedback from customers. It represents the overall satisfaction level of customers based on their responses.

   Formula: CSAT = (Number of Satisfied Customers / Total Number of Respondents) * 100

3. **Net Promoter Score (NPS):** Net Promoter Score is used to measure customer loyalty and the likelihood of customers recommending a business to others. It is based on responses to a specific question asking customers to rate their likelihood of recommending the business on a scale of 0-10.

   Formula: NPS = (%Promoters - %Detractors)

To calculate the percentages of promoters and detractors, respondents are categorized into three groups based on their ratings:

- Promoters: Customers who gave a rating of 9-10.
- Detractors: Customers who gave a rating of 0-6.
- Passives: Customers who gave a rating of 7-8.

The percentages are calculated as follows:
%Promoters = (Number of Promoters / Total Number of Respondents) * 100 %Detractors = (Number of Detractors / Total Number of Respondents) * 100

Finally, the NPS is determined by subtracting the percentage of detractors from the percentage of promoters.

Please note that these formulas provide a general understanding of how these metrics are calculated. In practice, there may be variations in the specific calculations or additional factors considered.

The purpose of promotional campaigns is to generate awareness and convert that awareness into interest. Promotional campaigns are designed to capture the attention of the target audience, increase their awareness of a product, service, or brand, and ultimately drive them to take action.

Here are the key purposes of promotional campaigns:

1. **Generate Awareness:** Promotional campaigns aim to create visibility and increase brand recognition among the target audience. By utilizing various marketing channels and strategies, such as advertising, public relations, social media, and content marketing, the campaign seeks to reach a wide audience and make them aware of the product, service, or brand.

2. **Build Interest:** Once the audience becomes aware of the offering, the promotional campaign aims to generate interest and curiosity. This can be achieved by highlighting unique features, benefits, or value propositions that differentiate the product or service from competitors. The goal is to capture the audience's attention and make them interested in learning more.

3. **Drive Engagement:** Promotional campaigns encourage audience engagement by providing opportunities for interaction and involvement. This can include interactive content, contests, giveaways, or events that encourage the audience to actively participate and engage with the brand. By fostering engagement, the campaign aims to deepen the audience's interest and create a sense of connection with the offering.

4. **Generate Leads:** One of the key purposes of promotional campaigns is to generate leads,

which are potential customers who have shown interest in the offering. The campaign may include lead generation tactics such as capturing email addresses, offering free trials or demos, or providing gated content that requires contact information for access. The goal is to convert interested individuals into leads that can be further nurtured through targeted marketing efforts.

5. **Convert to Sales:** Ultimately, the primary purpose of promotional campaigns is to drive conversions and generate sales. The campaign aims to influence the audience's decision-making process and encourage them to make a purchase or take a desired action, such as signing up for a service, making a reservation, or placing an order. By effectively communicating the value and benefits of the offering, the campaign seeks to convert interested individuals into paying customers.

In summary, promotional campaigns play a vital role in creating awareness, generating interest, and ultimately converting prospects into customers. Strategically designing and executing promotional activities can enable businesses to effectively reach their target audience, build brand visibility, and drive desired actions that contribute to growth.

Now that we have explored various sales and marketing strategies, it's time to dive into the sales process itself. Whether you're selling a product, a service, or an idea, understanding, and mastering the four steps of the sales process is crucial for success.

These steps are: probing, empathizing, proving, and closing. Let's take a closer look at each step:

Probing:

The first step in the sales process is probing, which involves asking insightful questions to gather information about the customer's needs, challenges, and desires. This step is crucial for understanding the customer's situation and identifying how your product or service can provide value and solve their problems. Effective probing requires active listening and the ability to ask open-ended questions that encourage the customer to share their thoughts and concerns.

Empathizing:

After gathering information through probing, the next step is empathizing. This step involves putting yourself in the customer's shoes and understanding their emotions, motivations, and perspectives. By showing genuine empathy and understanding, you can build rapport and establish trust with the customer. Empathizing allows you to connect with the customer on a deeper level and demonstrate that you genuinely care about their needs and goals.

Proving:

Once you have gathered information and established empathy, it's time to move on to proving. This step involves presenting the features, benefits, and value of your product or service in a compelling way. Use persuasive techniques, such as storytelling or providing social proof, to demonstrate how your offering can address the customer's specific needs and deliver tangible results. Utilize sample tables, case studies, or formulas to showcase the effectiveness and success of your solution. The goal is to provide evidence that your product or service is the best choice for the customer.

Closing:

The final step in the sales process is closing the deal. This step involves asking for the customer's commitment and sealing the agreement. It's essential to be confident, clear, and persuasive during the closing stage. Use closing techniques, such as offering incentives or creating a sense of urgency, to encourage the customer to take action. Ensure that all the customer's concerns and objections have been addressed throughout the process and be prepared to negotiate if necessary. The goal is to secure a mutually beneficial agreement that satisfies the customer's needs and achieves your sales objectives.

By understanding and implementing these four steps of the sales process—probing, empathizing, proving, and closing—you can navigate the sales journey with confidence and increase your chances of success. Each step is interconnected and builds upon the previous ones. With practice and refinement, you can become a skilled sale professional capable of driving business growth and forging lasting customer relationships.

Now that we have explored the sales process and its integration with sales and marketing strategies, you are equipped with a comprehensive toolkit to excel in the dynamic world of sales and marketing. Embrace these strategies, master the sales process, and unleash your creativity to make a significant impact on your target audience and achieve your business goals.

Resources:

- Traditional Advertising Platforms: Explore traditional advertising platforms such as newspapers, radio stations, television networks, and outdoor advertising providers. Local San Diego options include The San Diego Union-Tribune, iHeartMedia San Diego, NBC San Diego, and Lamar Advertising San Diego.
- Social Media Marketing Tools: Utilize social media management tools like Hootsuite, Buffer, and Sprout Social to streamline your social media marketing efforts and efficiently manage multiple platforms.
- SEO Resources: Access SEO resources like Moz, SEMrush, and Ahrefs to enhance your website's visibility in search engine results and optimize your online presence.
- PR and Media Outreach Guides: Learn about effective PR and media outreach strategies from resources like "The New Rules of Marketing and PR" by David Meerman Scott and "Media Relations Guidebook" by Sheila M. Cannon.
- CRM Software: Explore popular CRM software options such as Salesforce, HubSpot CRM, and Zoho CRM to streamline your customer management processes and enhance customer relationships.

Case Study - Artistic Expressions:

Artistic Expressions is a small art gallery based in San Diego, specializing in showcasing local artists' works. Here are the sequential steps taken by Artistic Expressions in their sales and marketing strategies:

Step 1: **Traditional Advertising and Promotion:** Artistic Expressions utilized local newspapers, radio stations, and outdoor billboards to promote their gallery's grand opening event, highlighting the unique artworks on display.

Step 2:   **Social Media and Content Marketing:** The gallery established a strong presence on Instagram and Facebook, regularly posting high-quality images of featured artworks, behind-the-scenes glimpses, and artist spotlights. They encouraged user-generated content by organizing contests and hashtags related to their gallery.

Step 3:   **SEO and Online Advertising:** Artistic Expressions optimized their website with relevant keywords, meta tags, and engaging content to improve their search engine rankings. They also ran targeted online ads on platforms like Google Ads and Facebook Ads to reach art enthusiasts in the San Diego area.

Step 4:   **Public Relations and Media Outreach:** The gallery collaborated with local art bloggers and influencers to gain media exposure. They hosted exclusive art events for journalists and media personnel, resulting in positive reviews and feature articles in local publications.

Step 5: **Customer Relationship Management:** Artistic Expressions implemented a CRM system to track customer preferences and purchase history. They sent personalized email newsletters to their subscriber base, informing them about upcoming art exhibits, artist talks, and exclusive promotions.

Conclusion:

Developing a comprehensive sales and marketing strategy is essential to effectively reach your target audience, build brand awareness, and cultivate strong customer relationships. In combining traditional advertising, social media marketing, SEO, public relations, and CRM strategies, you'll create a robust framework that drives business growth. Embrace the vibrant and creative culture of San

Diego as you implement these strategies and watch your business thrive.

And now, a marketing joke:

Why did the marketer bring a beach towel to the brainstorming session?

Because they wanted to soak up all the creative waves!

Chapter 6: Delivering Exceptional Customer Service

Greetings, customer service enthusiasts! Welcome to Chapter 6, where we strive to deliver nothing less than exceptional customer service. Now, you may have heard the saying, "Is the customer always right?" Well, buckle up and get ready to discover the truth behind this age-old question.

In this chapter, we'll delve into the intricacies of creating memorable customer experiences and tracking the ever-important Net Promoter Score (NPS). We'll unravel the secrets to turning satisfied customers into raving fans and leveraging the power of word-of-mouth growth.

Allow me to share a little story from my days as a Bank Manager at Union Bank. Picture this: a bustling branch filled with a diverse and talented staff, each representing the vibrant community we served. We understood that exceptional customer service wasn't just about smiling faces and warm greetings—it was about truly connecting with our clients, understanding their unique needs, and going above and beyond to exceed their expectations.

Together with our bank branch team, we would huddle up, brainstorming, and customizing our service delivery to cater to each individual. We knew that the key to success lay in listening attentively, addressing concerns promptly, and providing personalized solutions. Our aim was to create such remarkable experiences that our clients couldn't help but become enthusiastic brand ambassadors.

By tracking this valuable metric, we were able to gauge customer satisfaction, identify areas for improvement, and unlock the secret to continuous growth. After all, word-of-mouth recommendations are a powerful force that can propel any business to new heights.

So, my fellow customer service aficionados, get ready to unleash your inner service superstar. Together, let's uncover the secrets to delivering exceptional customer service, creating lasting connections, and turning customers into devoted fans. Exceptional service is not just about meeting expectations—it's about going above and beyond to surprise and delight. Are you ready to join the ranks of customer service champions? Let's splash and make waves in the ocean of outstanding service!

And now, without further ado, let the strut toward exceptional customer service begin!

Delivering Exceptional Customer Service: The Customer Reigns Supreme:

In today's competitive business landscape, delivering exceptional customer service is paramount to success. In this chapter, you will need to explore strategies and techniques to understand your customer's needs, build customer loyalty and retention, handle customer complaints and feedback effectively, and measure customer satisfaction and success. Prioritizing customer service and creating a positive customer experience can cultivate strong relationships, foster repeat business, and earn a stellar reputation in San Diego's vibrant market.

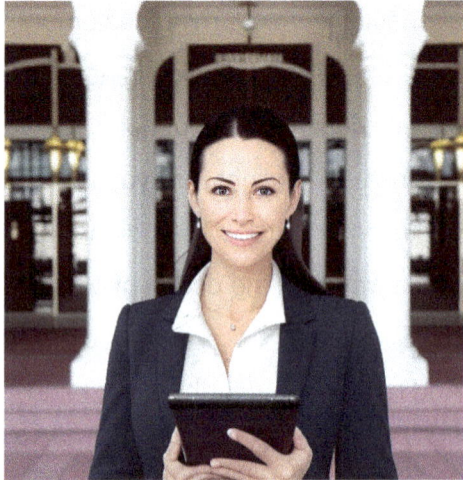

Understanding Your Customers' Needs:

To deliver exceptional customer service, you must first understand your customers' needs. You will need to research methods for conducting market research, gathering customer insights, and analyzing data to gain a deep understanding of your target audience. In identifying their pain points, preferences, and expectations, you can tailor your products, services, and interactions to meet and exceed their needs.

Building Customer Loyalty and Retention:

Loyal customers are the lifeblood of any successful business. Seek strategies to build customer loyalty and foster long-term relationships. From personalized communication and loyalty programs to exceptional after-sales support and customer appreciation initiatives, you will need to implement actionable tips to turn satisfied customers into brand advocates who keep coming back for more.

Handling Customer Complaints and Feedback:

Even the best businesses encounter occasional customer complaints or negative feedback. You will need to learn effective techniques for handling customer complaints and turning them into opportunities for improvement. By responding empathetically, resolving issues promptly, and using customer feedback as valuable insights, you can enhance your products, services, and overall customer experience.

Measuring Customer Satisfaction and Success:

Measuring customer satisfaction is crucial to gauge the effectiveness of your customer service efforts. Explore different methods and tools to collect feedback, conduct surveys, and analyze customer satisfaction metrics. By monitoring key performance indicators (KPIs) and continuously striving for improvement, you can ensure that your customers' needs are met, and their expectations are exceeded.

Resources:
• CustomerThink - https://customerthink.com/ - An online community and resource center for customer-centric professionals, providing articles, case studies, and insights on customer service and satisfaction.
• Zendesk - https://www.zendesk.com/resources/ - A resource hub offering whitepapers, webinars, and guides on customer service best practices and strategies.
• Qualtrics - https://www.qualtrics.com/customer-experience/ - A platform that provides tools and resources for measuring and improving customer experience, including survey templates and CX guides.
• Market Research Tools: Utilize tools such as SurveyMonkey, and Google Surveys to gather customer insights, conduct surveys, and analyze data.
• Customer Relationship Management (CRM) Software: Implement CRM software solutions like Salesforce, HubSpot CRM, and Zoho CRM to effectively manage customer relationships, track interactions, and personalize customer experiences.

- **Customer Feedback and Review Platforms:** Leverage customer feedback and review platforms such as Yelp, Google My Business, and Trustpilot to gather feedback, respond to reviews, and enhance your online reputation.
- **Customer Satisfaction Measurement Tools:** Utilize customer satisfaction measurement tools like Net Promoter Score (NPS), Customer Effort Score (CES), and Customer Satisfaction Score (CSAT) surveys to assess customer satisfaction levels and identify areas for improvement.
- **Customer Service Training Resources:** Access training resources like "Delivering Happiness" by Tony Hsieh and "Customer Service Training 101" by Renee Evenson to develop customer service skills within your team and create a customer-centric culture.

Case Study - Surf 'n' Sand Vacation Rentals:

Surf 'n' Sand Vacation Rentals is a small vacation rental management company in San Diego that prioritizes exceptional customer service. Here are the sequential steps taken by Surf 'n' Sand Vacation Rentals to deliver exceptional customer service:

Step 1: **Understanding Your Customers' Needs:** The company conducted surveys and

collected feedback from guests to understand their vacation preferences, expectations, and desired amenities. This helped them curate a portfolio of rental properties that catered to various customer needs, from beachfront condos to family-friendly homes.

Step 2: **Building Customer Loyalty and Retention:** Surf 'n' Sand Vacation Rentals implemented a loyalty program for repeat guests, offering exclusive discounts, personalized recommendations, and priority booking privileges. They also maintained regular communication with their guests through personalized emails and newsletters.

Step 3: **Handling Customer Complaints and Feedback:** The company established a dedicated customer support team that promptly addressed any issues or complaints raised by guests. They followed a proactive approach to resolve problems and ensure a positive guest experience. Guest feedback was used to improve their services, enhance property listings, and provide better amenities.

Step 4: **Measuring Customer Satisfaction and Success:** Surf 'n' Sand Vacation Rentals regularly measured customer satisfaction by sending post-stay surveys to guests. They tracked key metrics like NPS, CES, and CSAT scores to gauge guest satisfaction levels and identify areas for improvement. This data helped them make informed decisions and continuously enhance their customer service.

By following these steps, Surf 'n' Sand Vacation Rentals established a reputation for delivering exceptional customer service, leading to positive reviews, repeat bookings, and increased referrals.

Conclusion:

Delivering exceptional customer service is a vital aspect of running a successful business. An understanding of your customers' needs helps build loyalty, effectively handle complaints, and measure satisfaction. This way you can create a memorable customer experience that sets you apart from the competition. Implement the strategies and utilize the resources mentioned in this chapter to deliver exceptional customer service and build lasting relationships with your customers in San Diego and beyond.

And now, a customer service joke:

Why did the Ocean provide exceptional customer service?

Because it's always ready to make a splash.

Chapter 7: Operational Efficiency and Productivity

Now, before we dive into the nitty-gritty, let me tell you a little secret: efficiency and productivity are not always two peas in a pod. Intrigued? Well, buckle up and get ready for an exciting chapter!

In this chapter, we'll explore the delicate balance between efficiency and productivity, understanding that they are not one and the same. We'll delve into the world of Key Performance Indicators (KPIs) and uncover the metrics that truly measure success and drive improvement.

But first, let's take a little detour to the unforgettable year of 2020. Ah, yes, the pandemic era, where efficient technologies became our lifelines, allowing us to stay connected and productive from the comfort of our homes. However, here's the twist: while efficiency soared, productivity took a hit. Why, you ask? Well, it turns out that social interactions, those seemingly unproductive moments of connection, played a vital role in keeping our gears turning smoothly.

Think about it—a classroom full of students, exchanging ideas, sharing laughter, and sparking creativity. Those spontaneous interactions, though seemingly inefficient, actually fueled productivity in ways that virtual meetings couldn't replicate. So, let's take a moment to appreciate the power of human connection in the pursuit of productivity.

Now, let's fast forward to the present, where we understand that our workforce plan should embrace flexibility. We've learned that rigid structures can stifle productivity, while a harmonious blend of autonomy and collaboration can lead to astonishing results. So, get ready to explore the strategies that optimize operational efficiency and foster a productive work environment.

But wait, there's more! We can't talk about operational efficiency without addressing the logistics challenges of the pandemic era. While the world seemed to turn upside down, our inventory controls kept us on track, ensuring that we met our clients' demands with confidence and grace.

So, my fellow efficiency enthusiasts, let's engage in operational excellence, where efficiency and productivity dance to their unique tunes. To unlock the secrets of continuous improvements, embrace the value of human interactions, and craft a workforce plan that champions flexibility. Get ready to unleash the full potential of your operations and witness the remarkable results that await.

Remember, it's not just about being efficient—it's about striking the perfect balance that fuels productivity and drives success. Are you ready to revolutionize your operations? Let's jump in and make waves in the sea of operational excellence!

Operational Efficiency and Productivity: Streamlining Success for Maximum Results:

To run a successful small business in San Diego, you will need to master the art of operational efficiency and productivity. By effectively managing your resources, optimizing processes, and embracing technology, you can ensure smooth operations and maximize productivity. Explore key areas such as supply chain management, inventory control, business process optimization, technology solutions, workforce planning, and productivity monitoring. It is important to research, learn, and understand the information presented here to apply it to your business.

Supply Chain Management and Inventory Control:

Efficient supply chain management and inventory control are critical for seamless operations. You will need to research methods to streamline your supply chain, manage inventory levels, and ensure timely deliveries. Establishing strong relationships with suppliers and implementing inventory management systems are some approaches you can explore to optimize your supply chain and meet customer demand efficiently.

Streamlining Business Processes:

Streamlining your business processes can lead to improved efficiency and reduced costs. Research process mapping and analysis techniques to identify bottlenecks, eliminate redundancies, and enhance workflow. Streamlining your operations can save time, resources, and deliver products or services more efficiently to your customers.

Leveraging Technology Solutions:

Technology plays a vital role in enhancing operational efficiency. Explore various technology solutions such as project management tools, automation software, and cloud-based systems. By leveraging technology effectively, you can automate repetitive tasks, improve communication, and increase overall productivity in your business.

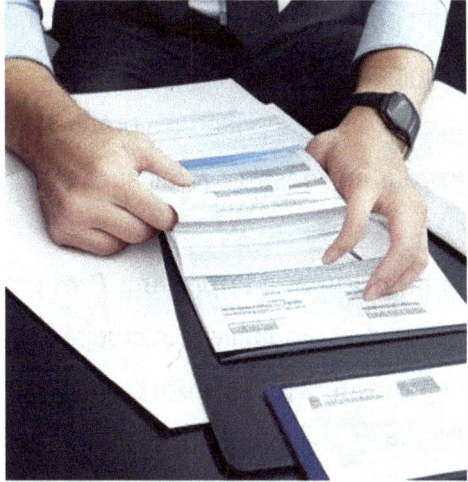

Workforce Planning and Management:

A well-managed workforce is essential for operational efficiency. Make time to research effective workforce planning strategies, talent acquisition approaches, and employee training and performance management techniques. Your efforts in ensuring the right people are in the right roles, providing ongoing training, and fostering a positive work culture, can optimize your workforce's productivity and contribute to your business's overall success.

Monitoring and Improving Productivity:
Monitoring productivity is crucial to identify areas for improvement and ensure optimal performance. Research key productivity metrics, tracking methods, and performance evaluation techniques. Through productivity measurements, realistic goals, and strategic efficiency, you can continuously enhance your business's performance and drive growth.

Resources:
• Supply Chain Management Tools: Explore supply chain management tools like SAP SCM, Oracle SCM Cloud, and JDA Supply Chain to optimize your supply chain operations.
• Inventory Management Systems: Implement inventory management systems such as TradeGecko, Zoho Inventory, and Fishbowl to efficiently manage your inventory and streamline order fulfillment processes.

• Business Process Mapping Tools: Utilize process mapping tools like Lucidchart, Microsoft Visio, and Gliffy to visualize and analyze your business processes, identifying areas for improvement.
• Project Management Software: Use project management software such as Asana, Trello, or Monday.com to streamline project workflows, collaborate with your team, and track progress.
• Workforce Planning Resources: Access resources like "Effective Workforce Planning: A Guide for Small Businesses" and "Strategic Workforce Planning: Guidance & Back-Up Plans" to develop effective workforce planning strategies.
• Productivity Monitoring Tools: Utilize productivity monitoring tools such as RescueTime, Toggl, or Time Doctor to track employee productivity, identify time wastage, and improve efficiency.

Case Study - Cafe San Diego:

Cafe San Diego is a small coffee shop located in downtown San Diego. Here are the sequential steps taken by Cafe San Diego to enhance operational efficiency and productivity:

Step 1: **Supply Chain Management and Inventory Control:** The cafe built strong relationships with local coffee bean suppliers to ensure a steady and timely supply. They implemented an inventory management system to track coffee bean stock, optimize ordering quantities, and reduce wastage.

Step 2:   **Streamlining Business Processes:** Cafe San Diego analyzed their processes, identified bottlenecks, and streamlined their workflow. They optimized their order-taking, preparation, and serving processes to minimize wait times and improve customer satisfaction.

Step 3:   **Leveraging Technology Solutions:** The cafe implemented a point-of-sale (POS)

system to automate transactions, track sales, and manage inventory. They also utilized social media platforms and online ordering systems to streamline customer interactions and increase online visibility.

Step 4: **Workforce Planning and Management:** Cafe San Diego focused on hiring skilled baristas and provided regular training to enhance their coffee-making skills. They established clear roles and responsibilities, fostering effective teamwork and communication among employees.

Step 5: **Monitoring and Improving Productivity:** The cafe tracked key productivity metrics such as the number of orders served per hour, customer wait times, and customer satisfaction ratings. They conducted regular performance evaluations and provided feedback to employees to improve their efficiency and productivity.

By implementing these strategies, Cafe San Diego achieved greater operational efficiency, improved customer service, and increased profitability.

Conclusion:

This chapter highlighted the importance of operational efficiency and productivity in running a successful small business. Managing the supply chain, streamlining business processes, harnessing technology, optimizing the workforce, and monitoring productivity can enhance the overall efficiency of your operations. Utilize the resources and tools mentioned in this chapter to implement strategies tailored to your business needs and maximize your business's potential in San Diego and beyond.

And now, it's time for a joke:

Why did the operational efficiency expert bring a calculator to the bakery?

To ensure they always got their just desserts!

Chapter 8: Human Resources and Risk Mitigation

Welcome to Chapter 8, where we enter the land of Human Resources and Risk Mitigation. Brace yourself for a fun and enlightening exploration of how we can create a diverse, inclusive, and welcoming environment while effectively managing operational risks.

As you reach the end of this chapter on designing job descriptions and mitigating operational risks, you now have the knowledge and tools to create clear expectations for your team members and protect your business from potential pitfalls. Remember, it is your responsibility to research, learn, and understand the information presented here to ensure its effective implementation in your organization.

Before we dive into the nitty-gritty of risk management, let's take a moment to appreciate the magic of a well-crafted Human Resources (HR) and Employee Manual. Picture this: a document that lays out the guidelines, policies, and expectations for everyone in your organization, creating a strong foundation of trust through transparency. It's like a roadmap that leads to a harmonious and productive work environment.

Moreover, the responsibility falls on you to research, learn, and understand the information presented in this chapter. As an entrepreneur, you must prioritize employee safety and implement protocols that ensure their well-being. Providing training and fostering a culture of care within your organization will contribute to the happiness and health of your workforce, which is essential for a successful enterprise.

Let's acknowledge that times are changing rapidly, with technology advancements and

automation becoming more prevalent. While machines can assist in lightening the load, they can never fully replace the value brought by human workers. Additionally, environmental risks persist, emphasizing the need for diligent risk management practices.

In today's workplace, there is an importance of cultivating a diverse and welcoming environment, where employees of all backgrounds can thrive and contribute their unique perspectives. Strategies for attracting and retaining top talent, as well as fostering an inclusive culture, should be addressed to celebrate diversity within your organization.

Furthermore, you can mitigate operational risks through Professional Employer Organizations (PEOs), enabling you to transfer certain risks and focus on building a thriving business. PEOs offer a comprehensive approach to risk management by providing outsourced human resources services. Through an effective partnership with a PEO, you can tap into their expertise in areas such as payroll administration, employee benefits, and compliance with employment laws and regulations. This partnership allows you to offload administrative burdens and mitigate risks associated with HR-related issues, enabling you to focus on your core business activities.

By leveraging insurance and PEOs, you can transfer certain operational risks to specialized entities that are equipped to handle them effectively. This risk transfer not only provides you with a safety net but also frees up your time and resources, allowing you to concentrate on what truly matters – building a thriving and successful business.

The success of your business depends on your ability to adapt, embrace diversity, and prioritize the well-being of your employees. With the knowledge gained in this chapter, you are well-equipped to navigate the challenges and create a safe and inclusive work environment.

Aim to design job descriptions that inspire, implement strategies that nurture a diverse and welcoming environment, and tackle operational risks head-on. Get ready to revolutionize your HR practices, create a culture of transparency and trust, and embrace the ever-changing landscape of risk management.

Human Resources and Talent Management: Nurturing a Dream Team for Success:

Let's delve into the critical aspects of human resources and risk mitigation for your small business. Running a business in San Diego necessitates your careful attention to operational risks, compliance with statutory regulations, effective risk assessment and management, risk transfer through insurance, and efficient management of payroll and human resources. The strategies outlined in this chapter will help protect your business, ensure compliance, and create a positive work environment for your employees.

Identifying and Mitigating Operational Risks:

To secure the long-term success of your business, you must identify and mitigate operational risks. This chapter will discuss the process of identifying potential risks specific to your industry and developing strategies to mitigate them. From conducting risk assessments to implementing safety protocols and contingency plans, it is important for you to proactively address risks and protect your business from potential disruptions.

Ensuring Compliance with Statutory Regulations:

Compliance with statutory regulations is essential to avoid legal issues and maintain a positive reputation for your business. This chapter will explore the key regulatory requirements in San Diego, including employment laws, health and safety regulations, and tax obligations. Understanding regulations and implementing necessary measures will enable compliance and minimize the risk of penalties or legal complications.

Effective Risk Assessment and Management:

Effective risk assessment and management are vital for mitigating potential risks. This chapter will guide you through the process of conducting risk assessments, identifying potential risks, and developing risk management strategies. By implementing a structured risk management framework and regularly reviewing and updating your risk management plan, you can proactively address risks and protect your business interests.

Transferring Risks through Insurance:

Insurance plays a crucial role in transferring and mitigating risks that your business may face. There are several types of insurance coverage you should consider, such as general liability insurance, professional liability insurance, and workers' compensation insurance. With a key partner, learn how to assess your insurance needs, select appropriate coverage, and work with insurance providers to ensure your business is adequately protected.

Utilizing Payroll Services and HR Resources:

Efficient management of payroll and human resources is essential for smooth business operations. This chapter will explore payroll service options, including outsourcing payroll functions to professional service providers. Additionally, we referenced the effectiveness of human resources management, including employee onboarding, training and development, performance evaluations, and maintaining a positive work culture.

Equipping yourself with knowledge and implementing the recommended strategies can help you confidently navigate the challenges of human resources and risk mitigation, ensuring your small business's success and growth.

Resources:
• Insurance Information Institute - https://www.iii.org/ - Providing information on different types of insurance coverage and risk management strategies.
• Professional Employer Organizations (PEOs) - https://www.napeo.org/ - Explore the benefits and services offered by PEOs to effectively manage human resources and mitigate employment-related risks.
• Occupational Safety and Health Administration (OSHA): Access OSHA's website for information on workplace safety regulations and guidelines specific to your industry. OSHA Website - https://www.osha.gov/
• Small Business Administration (SBA) Guide to Employment Laws: Refer to the SBA's comprehensive guide on employment laws to understand your obligations as an employer. SBA Guide - https://www.sba.gov/business-guide/manage-your-business/hire-manage-employees
• Insurance Brokers: Consult with insurance brokers like Marsh & McLennan Agency and Chambers & Company Insurance

Brokers to explore insurance coverage options for your business.
• Payroll Service Providers: Consider utilizing payroll service providers such as TriNet and ADP to streamline your payroll processes and ensure compliance.
• HR Resources: Access resources like sdshrm.org and sdeahr.org for valuable information on human resources management, including best practices for employee recruitment, training, and retention.

Case Study - Retail Boutique San Diego:

Retail Boutique San Diego is a small clothing store located in a popular shopping district in San Diego. Here are the sequential steps taken by Retail Boutique San Diego to manage human resources and mitigate risks:

Step 1:   **Identifying and Mitigating Operational Risks:** The boutique conducted a thorough risk assessment to identify potential risks, such as inventory theft, customer accidents, and supply chain disruptions. They implemented security measures, trained staff on safety protocols, and established relationships with reliable suppliers to mitigate these risks.

Step 2:   **Ensuring Compliance with Statutory Regulations:** The boutique familiarized itself with employment laws, including minimum wage requirements, anti-discrimination laws, and record-keeping obligations. They maintained accurate employee records, provided proper training, and established fair employment practices to ensure compliance.

Step 3:   **Effective Risk Assessment and Management:** Retail Boutique San Diego regularly reviewed and updated their risk management

plan. They conducted ongoing assessments to identify emerging risks and developed strategies to mitigate them, such as implementing a loss prevention program and monitoring customer feedback for potential issues.

Step 4: **Transferring Risks through Insurance:** The boutique obtained comprehensive general liability insurance to protect against property damage, bodily injury claims, and product liability. They also secured workers' compensation insurance to provide coverage for employee injuries or illnesses.

Step 5: **Utilizing Payroll Services and HR Resources:** Retail Boutique San Diego partnered with a payroll service provider to handle payroll processing, tax filings, and employee benefits administration. They also utilized online HR resources to access templates for employee contracts, policies, and performance evaluation forms.

By implementing these strategies, Retail Boutique San Diego effectively managed human resources, mitigated risks, and created a safe and compliant work environment.

Conclusion:

This chapter highlighted the significance of human resources management and risk mitigation for small businesses in San Diego. Identifying and managing operational risks, complying with statutory regulations,

conducting thorough risk assessments, utilizing insurance coverage, and leveraging payroll services and HR resources can safeguard your business and cultivate a harmonious work environment. Take advantage of the recommended resources to access valuable information and tools that will assist you in your human resources and risk management endeavors.

And now, a risky joke:

How many HR experts does it take to change a lightbulb?

One, but it takes six months to get approval from the committee.

Chapter 9: Financial Pro Forma

Ahoy, fellow entrepreneurs and financial adventurers! In this chapter, we will uncover the world of the Financial Pro Forma, where dreams are turned into numbers and goals are meant to be broken!

Imagine this: you, a fearless entrepreneur, armed with a vision and a spreadsheet, seeking a thrilling voyage of future revenues, cost of sales, operating expenses, and profit margins. It's like being an alchemist, turning raw data into a golden path toward success.

But hold your excitement, for this journey is not one to be taken lightly. Just like an immigrant forging a new path in a foreign land, we must understand the intricacies and calculations that lay before us. With the power of spreadsheets at our fingertips, we can calculate and project future growth with astonishing precision.

Let me regale you with a tale of an accounting director, a maestro of numbers, who orchestrated a symphony of budgets using a collaborative approach. Like a skilled conductor, they harmonized the departments and their financial goals, ensuring that each section of the orchestra played its part to perfection.

We must not forget that every successful financial plan requires a solid foundation built on accurate assumptions and meticulous attention to detail. The systems within our company must be integrated seamlessly, capturing every essential piece of information to paint a complete picture of our financial future.

And while budget forecasts are undoubtedly crucial, we must always keep our eyes on the grand prize: cash flow. It's like the lifeblood of our enterprise, keeping our operations running smoothly and our dreams alive.

So, my fellow financial adventurers, fasten your seatbelts, grab your calculators, and let's begin on this exhilarating knowledge of the Financial Pro

Forma. You can conquer financial challenges, break boundaries, and unlock the true potential of your entrepreneurial endeavors!

Remember, in this quest for financial triumphs, goals are meant to be achieved, and success knows no bounds. Let the numbers guide us, the spreadsheets empower us, and our unwavering determination propel us toward a future filled with endless possibilities and remarkable achievements!

Now, let's set sail toward the land of financial prosperity and conquer the seas of entrepreneurship with numbers as our compass and dreams as our destination!

And as a little joke to brighten your day: Why did the accountant break up with the mathematician? They found it too hard to count on each other!

Financial Pro Forma: Crunching the Numbers for Financial Triumph:

Welcome to Chapter 9! We're diving into the world of financial pro forma—a magical crystal ball that helps you predict the future financial success of your business. Think of it as your very own fortune teller, but with numbers instead of crystal balls. In this chapter, we'll unravel the secrets of financial pro forma and show you how to create projections that would make even the most skeptical investor's eyebrows raise.

Key Data in a Financial Pro Forma:

A financial pro forma is like a treasure trove of data that reveals the financial health of your business. Here are some key data points that will make your financial pro forma sparkle:

- **Monthly burn rate:** Because who doesn't love to keep track of how much money goes up in smoke each month? Just kidding, this is what you keep spending each month.

- **Breakeven point:** The magical moment when your revenue catches up to your expenses and your business stops playing the losing game. Time to put on your victory dance shoes!

- **Free cash flow:** It's like finding cash in the pocket of your old jeans—extra money that can be used to fuel your business's growth and dreams.

- **Profit margins:** The sweet nectar of success, showing how efficiently your business turns revenue into profit. Cha-ching!

- **Customer acquisition costs (CAC):** The price tag of winning over new customers. This helps you figure out if it costs more to woo a customer than to hire a skywriter to proclaim your love for them.

- **Customer lifetime value (CLTV):** How much love (or money) a customer brings to your business over their lifetime. Let's make sure they stick around for the long haul!

- **Net promoter score (NPS):** Are your customers raving fans or secret agents spreading bad vibes? Your NPS will give you the inside scoop.

- **Return on investment (ROI):** The financial high-five you get when a brilliant investment pays off. It's time to celebrate with a round of virtual confetti!

- **Annual sales**: The grand total of all your revenue in a year. The bigger, the better—just like that pile of nachos at the ballpark.

Creating a Financial Pro Forma:

Now that we've piqued your interest, here are some tips to create your financial pro forma:

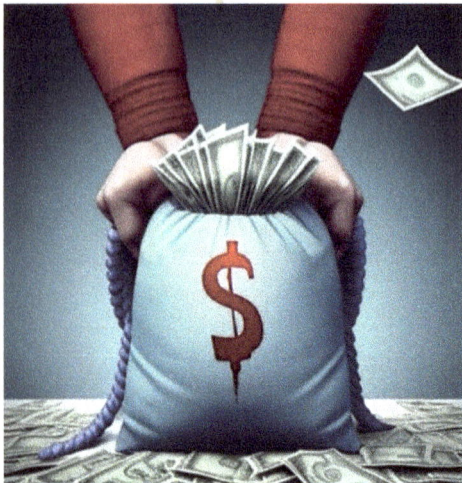

- **Be realistic:** Your financial pro forma should be more accurate than a fortune cookie prediction.

Keep your revenue expectations grounded and your expense estimates practical.

- **Use a spreadsheet:** Get those numbers dancing by using a spreadsheet template. Don't worry, you won't need any actual dance moves—unless you want to impress your calculator.

- **Get help from an expert:** If numbers make you break out in a cold sweat, enlist the assistance of an accountant or financial advisor. They'll be your financial fairy godmother (or godfather).

Financial Pro Forma Case Study: Sandy's Surf Shop

Let's take a look at how Sandy's Surf Shop, a small business in sunny San Diego, created its financial pro forma:

Step 1:   **Defining Assumptions:** Sandy's Surf Shop started by defining its revenue streams, estimating its monthly burn rate, and projecting its sales growth over the next three years.

Step 2:   **Revenue Projections:** Using market research and historical data, Sandy's Surf Shop projected their sales revenue for each product category and service they offer.

Step 3: **Expense Estimation**: Next, Sandy's Surf Shop identified its fixed and variable expenses, including rent, utilities, inventory costs, marketing expenses, and employee salaries.

Step 4: **Financial Statements**: Based on their revenue projections and expense estimations, Sandy's Surf Shop prepared its income statement, balance sheet, and cash flow statement for the next three years.

Step 5: **Analysis and Adjustments:** Sandy's Surf Shop analyzed its financial projections, adjusted its assumptions, and fine-tuned its numbers to ensure they were on their way to profitability.

Step 6: **Monitoring and Review:** Once their financial pro forma was in place, Sandy's Surf Shop regularly monitored their actual financial performance against their projections, making adjustments as needed.

Resources:
• Pro Forma Template - https://create.microsoft.com/en-us/template/business-expenses-budget-68cc5838-2d0b-4a87-93c1-29cd91ad7491:
• SBA Breakeven Point Calculator - https://www.sba.gov/breakevenpointcalculator/calculate/:

Conclusion:

With your financial pro forma in hand, you'll be equipped to make informed decisions, impress potential investors, and confidently navigate the financial landscape. Remember, the numbers don't lie—they're your business's magic mirror, reflecting its financial future. So, channel your inner wizard, crunch those numbers, and let your financial pro forma guide you toward a prosperous tomorrow!

Disclaimer: No crystal balls were harmed during the writing of this chapter.

Chapter 10: Small Business Lending and Grants

The moment you have been waiting for, where we delve into the exhilarating world of small business lending and grants. Get ready to unleash your inner Jerry Maguire as we shout together, "Show me the money!"

In the vibrant city of San Diego, where dreams are as big as the waves crashing against its beautiful shores, understanding the principles of creditworthiness and being loan-ready is the key to unlocking the financial resources that can fuel your entrepreneurial aspirations.

Picture this: you, a determined business owner, armed with a meticulously crafted business plan, stepping into the world of small business loans. You are ready to harness the power of your business plan to navigate the waters of the Small Business Administration (SBA) loan application process.

But let me take you back to a memory from my days as a bank manager, where I witnessed a parade of ill-prepared loan submissions. Oh, the horror! It was like watching a comedy of errors unfold before my eyes. However, these experiences taught me valuable lessons about the importance of thorough preparation and attention to detail when seeking financing.

Different businesses have different needs and securing the right type of lending for your specific purpose is crucial. Whether it's funding equipment purchases, expanding your operations, or boosting your working capital, understanding the diverse options available will empower you to make informed decisions that align with your business goals.

Now, while sales growth may make our hearts skip a beat, there's nothing quite like the sweet sound of free cash flow. This mighty force allows us to service our debt obligations, ensuring a stable financial foundation for our businesses to thrive upon.

So, my fellow financial adventurers, strap on your money-seeking goggles and get ready to explore the world of small business lending and grants. Being loan-ready is not just about having a compelling business plan but also about understanding the intricacies of creditworthiness and finding the right financial fit for your business.

And as a little San Diego-inspired joke to brighten your day: Why did the small business owner bring a ladder to the bank? Because they heard it was a high-interest account!

So, my fellow entrepreneurs, onward into Chapter 10 with enthusiasm and determination, ready to conquer the financial challenges and discover the treasure trove of small business lending and grants.

Show me the money, indeed!

Small Business Lending and Grants: Unleashing the Power of Capital:

Congratulations, you've made it to the financial superhero chapter! We're here to talk about small business lending and grants, the caped crusaders of financing options. Whether you're looking to expand your operations, purchase new equipment, or launch a daring new venture, securing the right funding can make all the difference. In this chapter, we'll explore the world of small business loans, specifically those offered by community lenders, and we'll also unveil a few grants that could be your business's secret weapon.

Just like how we geek out at Comic-Con, there are loan guarantee programs that can make lenders feel like they're in the front row of a blockbuster movie.

These programs help reduce the risk for lenders and make it easier for small businesses to secure financing, even when traditional options may seem as elusive as the last exclusive Funko Pop!

But hold on tight, heroes! SBA loans have their own requirements before you can wield their mighty power.

Let's take a look at some of the general requirements for an SBA loan:

1. Must be a for-profit entity: The SBA is all about supporting businesses that aim to save the day and turn a profit.
2. Must be in the United States: Our superhero powers are focused on businesses operating within the land of the free.
3. Must have been in operation for at least one year: Like seasoned heroes, the SBA wants to see that your business has battled through its first year.

4. Must have a good credit history: Superheroes earn their reputation, and a solid credit history shows your financial integrity.
5. Must provide collateral for the loan: Offering collateral is like providing a shield of protection for the lender.

Now, here's the inside scoop: the SBA isn't a direct lender. They're more like the Oracle of Delphi, providing guidance and insuring loans from banks. So, to harness the power of SBA loans, you'll need to team up with a lender, such as a bank or a Community Development Financial Institution (CDFI). They'll be your trusty sidekick in navigating the loan process.

Let's talk about some of the most common SBA loan programs:

1. 7(a) Loan Program: The superhero of SBA loans, offering loans up to $5 million for various business purposes. It's like having the Infinity Gauntlet of financing options.

2. 504 Loan Program: This program allows loans up to $5.5 million for fixed asset purchases, like real estate and equipment. It's your secret weapon for building a solid foundation for your business.

3. CDC/504 Loan Program: Similar to the 504 Loan Program but designed for businesses in rural areas. It's like having a hidden power that supports local businesses.

4. Microloan Program: For those who need smaller loans, this program offers loans up to $50,000 for small businesses with fewer than 500 employees. It's like a miniaturized hero with big possibilities.

But wait, there's more! When applying for an SBA loan, you'll need to gather a superhero ensemble of documentation, including:

- **Updated Business Plan:** A well-crafted plan that showcases your business's potential. Think of it as your secret superhero origin story.

- **Personal Financial Statement:** An overview of your personal financial situation. It's like revealing your hidden identity to the lenders.

- **Business Financial Statements:** Detailed information on your business's finances. These financial statements will be your trusty sidekick in proving your business's financial health.

- **Universal Debt Schedule:** A listing of all personal and business debts. It's like mapping out your past battles with creditors.

- **Collateral Information:** Documentation on the collateral you'll provide for the loan. Think of it as equipping yourself with armor to protect the lender's investment.

- **Loan Application:** The formal application specifies the loan amount, purpose, and terms. It's like crafting a mission brief for your lender.

- **Employment Verification:** Details on your employment history. It's like giving your lender a glimpse into your trusted team.

- **Tax Returns:** Documentation of your tax returns for the past two years. It's like unveiling your financial identity to the lenders.
- **Other Documentation:** Lenders may request additional documents to support your application. These extra documents are like hidden artifacts that reveal more about your business.

With the support of a trusted lender, you'll be well on your way to overcoming obstacles and achieving your business goals.

Section 2: Unleashing the Power of Loan Guarantee Programs in San Diego

Just like how we explore the exhilarating world of Comic-Con pop culture, let's dive into the loan guarantee programs available right here in sunny San Diego. These programs can make lenders feel like they're part of an epic superhero team-up, reducing their risk and helping small businesses secure financing with super ease!

1. CalCAP (California Capital Access Program): CalCAP is like the superhero of loan guarantee programs, swooping in to provide financing options to small businesses. Teaming up with local lenders, it offers guarantees that give them the confidence to support businesses that have been operating in California for at least two years.

Some of the San Diego-based lenders that join forces with CalCAP include:

- Bank of Southern California: They're like the Iron Man of lenders, using their financial prowess to support businesses.
- CDC Small Business Finance: As strategic as Captain America, they stand ready to provide financing solutions to businesses in need.
- Seacoast Commerce Bank: Like the Black Widow of lending, they're agile and

always ready to help businesses overcome challenges.

- Pacific Premier Bank: With the strength of the Hulk, they provide robust financing options to unleash your business's potential.

2. IBank (Infrastructure and Economic Development Bank): Like how superheroes protect the underdog, IBank focuses on lending guarantees for small businesses in low-income communities across the Golden State. It's like having a comic book origin story that empowers lenders to provide financing options to businesses that contribute to economic development. When it comes to IBank in San Diego, some of the local lenders that come to the rescue include:

- San Diego County Credit Union: Like the Flash, they're lightning-fast in offering financial support to local businesses.

- California Bank & Trust: With the precision of Hawkeye, they aim to hit the bullseye of your financing needs.
- Pacific Western Bank: As versatile as Spider-Man, they offer flexible loan options that adapt to your business's requirements.
- Mission Federal Credit Union: Like the X-Men, they're a force to be reckoned with, providing loans to help your business thrive.

In addition to these loan guarantee programs, there are also Community Development Financial Institution (CDFI) lenders that fight for financial justice in San Diego. These CDFIs provide access to affordable financing options, catering to underserved communities and businesses. For a comprehensive list of CDFIs visit ofn.org.

Some CDFIs serving the San Diego area include:

- Accessity San Diego: They're like the Robin Hood of lenders, aiming to level the playing field for small businesses.
- Pacific Community Ventures: Like the Guardians of the Galaxy, they're on a mission to support businesses and communities in need.
- Opportunity Fund: With the spirit of Shazam, they empower businesses with financial strength and guidance.

So, whether you're dressed as a superhero or a beloved character from your favorite comic book series, don't forget to explore these loan guarantee programs and connect with San Diego-based lenders, including the mighty CDFIs. They're here to help you secure the financing you need to turn your business aspirations into a heroic reality.

Reach out to these lenders and find out more about their specific loan programs, terms, and application processes. With their support, you'll be one step closer to achieving your business goals and writing a success story that would make even the biggest Comic-Con fan cheer!

Section 3: Unleashing the Power of Grants for Small Businesses

In addition to loans, grants can be an incredible superpower for small businesses. While they may not be as widely available as loans, grants offer free money that doesn't need to be repaid. It's like finding a hidden treasure chest filled with gold!

Here are some grants to consider:

1. The Freed Fellowship Grant: A monthly grant for black-owned businesses. Freed Fellowship Grant - https://www.freedfellowship.com/grant1
2. The Get Index Small Business Sweepstakes: A prize for one lucky small business. Get Index Small Business Sweepstakes - https://getindex.com/smallbizsweepstakes

3. The Awesome Foundation: Grants for small, innovative projects. Application deadlines vary. Awesome Foundation Grant - https://www.awesomefoundation.org/en/submissions/new

4. The Sky's the Limit Friends and Family Fund: Financial assistance for women and minority-owned small businesses. Sky's the Limit Friends and Family Fund - https://www.skysthelimit.org/friends-and-family

5. The Jobber Pro Grant: Financial assistance for businesses using Jobber Pro scheduling software. Deadline. Jobber Pro Grant

6. American Express Open Forum Grant: Grants for small businesses that are members of American Express Open Forum. American Express Open Forum Grant - https://www.americanexpress.com/en-us/company/corporate-sustainability/community-impact/backing-small/

7. Google for Startups Black Founders Fund: Grants for Black-owned startups. Google for Startups Black Founders Fund - https://startup.google.com/programs/black-founders-fund/united-states/

8. Microsoft BizSpark LaunchPad: Grants and access to Microsoft resources for early-stage startups. Microsoft BizSpark LaunchPad - https://www.microsoft.com/en-us/startups

9. The SoGal Foundation: Cash grants for Black women and Black nonbinary entrepreneurs. The SoGal Foundation - https://www.iamsogal.com/black-founder-startup-grant/

Case Study: Serenity Haven Spa

Sara was ready to unleash her entrepreneurial superpowers and secure a small business loan.

Step 1: **The Vision Awakens**: With her heart filled with passion and a vision of relaxation and rejuvenation, Sara envisioned new services that would new patrons. She quickly determined the use of funds.

Step 2:   **Assembling the Heroes**: Sara assembled a team of financial superheroes, including a trusted accountant and a knowledgeable small business advisor. Together, they reviewed her financial statements, ensuring that her profits were solid and her cash flow was sufficient to take on a loan and repay it without endangering her spa's stability.

Step 3:   **Unveiling the Business Plan:** Sara crafted a powerful business plan that demonstrated how the new services would

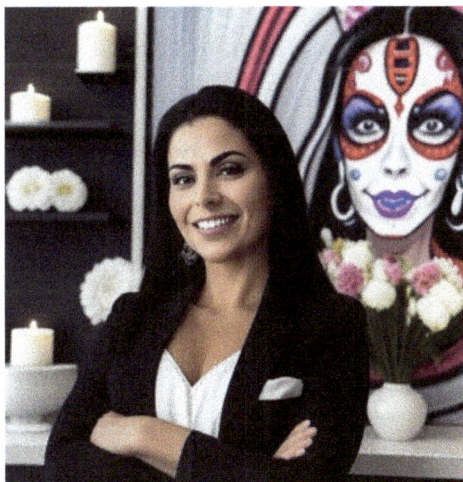

generate additional revenue and attract a wider customer base, all while maintaining the spa's exceptional quality and customer experience.

Step 4: **Conquering the Lending Realm:** Armed with her impeccable credit score, financial statements, and a compelling business plan, Sara approached lenders who specialized in small business loans.

Step 5: **Launching into Success:** With the loan secured, Sara launched her spa's expansion with a grand celebration.

Conclusion:

As you venture into the possibilities of small business lending and grants, remember that financial superheroes come in many forms. SBA loans can provide the backing you need to unleash your business's potential, while grants can provide that extra boost to help you reach new heights.

With the right funding on your side, your small business can conquer any challenge that comes its way. Now go out there and write the next chapter of your heroic business journey!

Disclaimer: No capes were harmed during the writing of this chapter.

Chapter 11: Using Accounting Software

Welcome to Chapter 11, where we balance the space of accounting software, guided by our friendly robotic assistants. In this futuristic landscape, these intelligent beings are here to assist us in our quest for financial order and strategic growth. As we explore the principles of accounting and delve into the intricacies of setting up and using accounting software, discover the immense power it holds in shaping the future of our businesses. So, fasten your seatbelts and join us on this adventure as we say, "We are here in peace" to the world of accounting!

Before we dive into the technical aspects of accounting software, it is essential to understand the underlying principles that govern the world of finance. Accounting principles provide a framework for recording, analyzing, and interpreting financial data. By adhering to these principles, businesses can ensure accuracy, transparency, and consistency in their financial reporting. This solid foundation is crucial for making informed business decisions and formulating strategies for growth.

Accurate accounting serves as the cornerstone for strategic growth. Businesses can gain valuable insights into their performance, identify trends, and make informed decisions. From tracking revenue and expenses to monitoring cash flow and profitability, accurate accounting data empowers CEOs and business leaders to identify opportunities and allocate resources.

As a new CEO, I once encountered a daunting challenge when I inherited a software company grappling with lousy cash flow management. The company was on the brink of sinking, with a lack of visibility into its financial position and insufficient controls in place.

Realizing the urgency, I recognized the dire need for accurate and reliable accounting practices to regain control and steer the company toward success. It was through the implementation of effective accounting systems and meticulous cash flow management that we were able to stabilize the company and set it on a path to prosperity.

When setting up an accounting system, businesses have the choice between managing their accounting processes in-house or outsourcing them to specialized accounting firms. Each option has its pros and cons, and the decision ultimately depends on factors such as budget, expertise, and the complexity of the business's financial operations. In-house accounting offers greater control and customization, while outsourced accounting can provide access to specialized knowledge and cost-effective solutions. It's crucial to weigh these factors and choose the option that best aligns with the business's needs and goals.

Setting up and Using Accounting Software: Balancing the Books with Technological Precision:

In this chapter, we'll explore the world of accounting software and its crucial role in efficiently managing your business's financial activities. Embracing the power of technology, accounting software acts as a financial ally, simplifying your bookkeeping tasks and offering valuable insights into your business's financial well-being. Regardless of whether you're a budding startup or a seasoned business, the process of selecting and setting up the right accounting software is vital for achieving financial success. Join us as we navigate through the sequential steps of choosing and configuring an accounting system tailored to meet your unique requirements.

Step 1:   **Assessing Business Needs:** The first step in setting up your accounting software is to assess your business's unique requirements. By identifying your invoicing, expense tracking, and financial reporting needs, you can narrow down the options and choose software that aligns with your goals.

Step 2:   **Researching Accounting Software Options:** Once you understand your business needs, it's time to explore the available accounting software options. Conduct thorough research, considering factors such as cost, features, user-friendliness, scalability, and integration capabilities. Shortlist a few software solutions that best fit your requirements.

Step 3:   **Evaluating the Options:** Evaluate the shortlisted accounting software options based on your specific needs. Consider your budget, the complexity of your financial operations, and the growth potential of your business.

This evaluation will help you make an informed decision on which software is the most suitable for your organization.

Step 4:   **Configuration and Setup Once:** you've chosen your accounting software, it's time to configure and set it up according to your business's specifications. Enter your business information, tax identification numbers, and customize the chart of accounts to reflect your revenue and expense categories. Set up tax rates applicable to your location to ensure accurate calculations.

Step 5:   **Data Migration and Integration:** If you've been using another system or spreadsheets to track your financial transactions, migrating your data to the new accounting software is crucial. Ensure a seamless transition by carefully importing your financial data, maintaining accuracy and completeness. Explore integration options with other tools you use, such as point-of-sale systems or inventory management software, to streamline data flow and enhance efficiency.

Step 6:   **Training and Familiarization:** To make the most of your accounting software, provide training sessions to your staff. Familiarize them with the software's key features and functionalities, including recording transactions, generating invoices, and running financial reports. Empower your team to leverage the software's capabilities and streamline their day-to-day financial tasks.

Step 7:   **Ongoing Monitoring and Maintenance:** With your accounting software set up and your team trained, it's time to embrace the power of technology in managing your financial activities. Establish a routine of monitoring the system regularly, reviewing financial reports, and reconciling accounts. Keep the software up to date with the latest updates and upgrades, taking advantage of new features that enhance efficiency.

Conclusion: Choosing and setting up the right accounting software is an essential step in effectively managing your business's finances. By following the sequential process outlined in this chapter, you can make informed decisions, configure the software to meet your specific needs, and streamline your financial operations. Embrace the power of technology and let accounting software be your trusted companion in navigating the complex world of business finance.

Resources:
• Wave - https://www.waveapps.com/ - A free accounting software known for its user-friendly interface and comprehensive features.
• Akaunting - https://akaunting.com/ - Another free accounting software that offers a range of modules and customization options.
• QuickBooks - https://quickbooks.intuit.com/pricing/ - A widely-used accounting software with both free and paid versions, offering advanced features and

As we bid farewell to this chapter on setting up and using accounting software, we leave behind the exciting world of numbers, ledgers, and robotic assistants. Through our experience, we have learned the importance of accurate accounting, the role it plays in strategic growth, and the various options available for managing our financial processes. Whether you choose to embrace the efficiency of in-house accounting or tap into the expertise of outsourced professionals, the key is to establish a robust system that aligns with your business goals.

The power of accounting software lies not only in its ability to streamline processes but also in the insights it provides for informed decision-making. Accurate financial data can enable you to navigate the business landscape with confidence, making sound choices that drive your organization forward.

Before we part ways, let's add a touch of humor to our financial journey with an accountant joke:

Why do accountants make great comedians?

Because they excel at delivering punchlines and balancing the books!

Congratulations on completing this comprehensive guidebook!

First and foremost, remember that entrepreneurship is a continuous learning process. The business landscape is ever evolving, and it is crucial to stay informed about industry trends, emerging technologies, and consumer preferences. Embrace new opportunities, remain adaptable, and be open to innovation as you navigate the dynamic world of entrepreneurship.

While financial success is an important measure of business achievement, true fulfillment lies in the impact you create in your community and the pursuit of your passion. Strive to make a difference, contribute to the betterment of society, and align your business with your values. By doing so, you can create a meaningful and purpose-driven enterprise.

Throughout your entrepreneurial journey, remember that failure is an inevitable part of the process. Embrace failures as valuable learning experiences and catalysts for growth. Maintain resilience, learn from your mistakes, and keep moving forward. Success often comes to those who persist despite obstacles.

Maintaining a healthy work-life balance is essential for long-term success. While running a business demands dedication and hard work, taking care of your physical and mental well-being is equally important. Make time for self-care, nurture relationships with loved ones, and find inspiration outside of work. Remember that your well-being directly contributes to the success of your business.

Finally, always remember the power of community and support. Surround yourself with mentors, fellow entrepreneurs, and industry professionals who can provide guidance, insights, and encouragement. Seek opportunities to collaborate, network, and learn from others. Together, we can create a thriving entrepreneurial ecosystem in San Diego and beyond.

With the knowledge, inspiration, and tools acquired from this book, you are well-prepared to embark on your entrepreneurial journey with confidence. Embrace the challenges, seize the opportunities, and make a lasting impact on your business. You have the potential to build America's finest businesses and leave a legacy. Best of luck on your remarkable entrepreneurial journey.

Appendix A: Sample Business Plan Template

A business plan serves as the blueprint for your small business, outlining your goals, strategies, and financial projections. Use this sample business plan template as a starting point for your plan:

Executive Summary:

- Business Value Proposition
- Target Market & Segment
- Products or Services
- Competitive Advantages
- Financial Projections
- Key Success Goals

The executive summary should be clear, concise, and persuasive. It should be short (1-2 pages) and make the reader want to see the rest of the business plan.

Company Description:

- Business History
- Legal Structure
- Industry
- Forecasted Trends

The company description should be comprehensive but not too detailed. It should describe the business structure and its potential.

Products or Services:

- Products or Services Themselves
- Benefits of the Products of Services
- How the Products or Services Align with the Target Market

The products or services section should be clear and informative. It should give a good description of what the business offers and the reason for the demand.

Market Analysis:

- Market Size
- Growth Potential
- Trends
- Competitive Landscape

The market analysis section should be thorough and insightful. It should state the industry and the business's position in the market and growth potential.

Marketing and Sales Strategy:

- Target market
- Marketing channels
- Marketing messages
- Sales goals

The marketing and sales strategy section should be detailed, specific, goal-oriented, and actionable. Show how the business plans to achieve its sales goals.

Organization and Management:

- Organizational structure
- Management team
- Roles and responsibilities of the management team

The organization and management section should be clear and concise.

Product Development and Operations:

- Product development process

- Operations process
- Quality control measures
- Inventory management
- Supplier relationships

The product development and operations section should be thorough and informative. Detail how the business creates and delivers its products or services.

Financial Projections:

- Sales forecast
- Profit and loss statement
- Cash flow statement
- Break-even analysis

The financial projections section should be realistic and achievable.

Funding Request:

- Amount of funding requested
- Use of funds
- Repayment terms

The funding request section should be clear and concise. It should give potential investors or lenders a good understanding of what the business needs and how it plans to repay the loan.

Appendices:

- Resumes of the management team
- Permits and licenses
- Contracts
- Financial statements

The appendices section should be organized and easy to reference.

Remember to customize this template to fit your specific business needs and industry. A comprehensive business plan will not only guide your business's growth but also impress potential investors or lenders.

Appendix B: Startup Cost Expenses

Starting a new business requires careful financial planning. Don't forget to list all your startup costs to estimate the initial expenses involved in launching your venture:

1. Pre-launch Expenses
   - Market research and feasibility studies
   - Business registration and legal fees
   - Permits and licenses
   - Professional services (accountant, attorney, etc.)
   - Insurance premiums
2. Equipment and Supplies
   - Office furniture and fixtures
   - Computers, software, and peripherals
   - Machinery or specialized equipment
   - Inventory or raw materials
   - Packaging and shipping supplies
3. Marketing and Branding
   - Logo and graphic design
   - Website development and hosting
   - Marketing collateral (business cards, brochures, etc.)
   - Advertising and promotional campaigns
   - Social media management
4. Operations
   - Rent or lease payments
   - Utilities and phone/internet services
   - Software subscriptions or licenses
5. Employee-related Costs
   - Salaries and wages
   - Payroll taxes and benefits
   - Training and development
   - Employee onboarding expenses
6. Miscellaneous Expenses
   - Travel and entertainment

- Professional memberships and subscriptions

These estimates may vary based on your industry, location, and business model. It's crucial to conduct research and consult with financial advisors to get accurate startup cost projections.

Appendix C: Hiring and Onboarding Checklist

When growing your team, it's important to have a systematic approach to hiring and onboarding. Use this checklist to ensure a smooth and effective process:

1. Pre-Hiring Phase
   - Define job requirements and responsibilities
   - Develop a job description and post job advertisements
   - Review resumes and shortlist candidates
   - Conduct pre-screening interviews
2. Interview and Selection
   - Schedule and conduct in-person or remote interviews
   - Prepare interview questions and assessments
   - Evaluate candidates based on skills, qualifications, and cultural fit
   - Check references and conduct background checks (if applicable)
   - Select the best candidate for the role
3. Offer and Negotiation
   - Extend a job offer to the selected candidate
   - Discuss compensation, benefits, and other terms
   - Handle negotiations professionally
   - Send a formal offer letter or employment contract
4. Onboarding Process
   - Prepare necessary paperwork (employment agreement, tax forms, etc.)
   - Set up employee files and record-keeping systems
   - Provide access to necessary tools, software, and equipment

- o   Schedule orientation and training sessions
- o   Introduce the new employee to the team and company culture
5. Training and Development
    - o   Create a training plan for the new employee
    - o   Assign mentors or trainers if needed
    - o   Provide access to training resources and materials
    - o   Monitor progress and provide ongoing support
6. Setting Expectations and Goals
    - o   Clearly communicate job expectations and performance standards
    - o   Set short-term and long-term goals with the employee
    - o   Schedule regular check-ins and performance evaluations
7. Employee Benefits and Administration
    - o   Enroll the employee in benefit programs (health insurance, retirement plans, etc.)
    - o   Provide information on company policies and procedures
    - o   Explain time-off and leave policies
    - o   Assist with completing necessary paperwork
8. Integration and Team Building
    - o   Encourage team members to welcome and support the new employee
    - o   Arrange social activities or team-building events
    - o   Foster a positive and inclusive work environment

Remember that effective onboarding is crucial for employee retention and productivity. Tailor this checklist to align with your specific company policies and procedures.

Appendix D: Marketing Plan Template

A well-defined marketing plan is essential for reaching your target audience and growing your business. Use this template as a guide to create your marketing plan:

1. Executive Summary
   - Overview of the marketing plan
   - Key goals and objectives
   - Target market and value proposition
2. Situation Analysis
   - Market analysis (industry trends, competition, target market)
   - SWOT analysis (strengths, weaknesses, opportunities, threats)
   - Customer analysis (demographics, psychographics, buying behavior)
3. Marketing Objectives
   - Specific, measurable, achievable, relevant, and time-bound (SMART) objectives
   - Examples: Increase brand awareness by X%, generate X leads per month, achieve X% market share
4. Target Market Strategy
   - Define your target market segments
   - Identify their needs, preferences, and pain points
   - Position your product or service to meet their needs
5. Value Proposition
   - Clearly articulate your unique selling points
   - Differentiate your business from competitors
   - Highlight the benefits and value your product or service provides
6. Marketing Tactics

- o Product strategy (features, pricing, packaging)
- o Distribution channels (online, retail, partnerships)
- o Promotional strategies (advertising, public relations, content marketing)
- o Digital marketing (website, social media, email marketing)
- o Offline marketing (events, direct mail, print media)
7. Budget and Resource Allocation
   - o Determine your marketing budget
   - o Allocate resources to different marketing tactics
   - o Monitor and track the return on investment (ROI) for each tactic
8. Implementation and Timeline
   - o Create a detailed timeline for executing marketing activities
   - o Assign responsibilities and deadlines
   - o Monitor progress and adjust as needed
9. Evaluation and Measurement
   - o Establish key performance indicators (KPIs)
   - o Regularly track and measure the effectiveness of marketing activities
   - o Analyze data and make data-driven decisions
10. Conclusion
    - o Summarize the key points of your marketing plan
    - o Reiterate the objectives and goals
    - o Outline the next steps for implementation

Adapt this template to fit your specific business and industry. Regularly review and update your marketing plan to stay aligned with market changes and business goals.

Appendix E: Customer Service Scripts & Templates

Consistent and effective customer service is crucial for building customer loyalty and satisfaction. Use these customer service scripts and templates as a starting point for handling common customer interactions:

1. Greeting Script (Phone)
   - "Thank you for calling [Company Name]. This is [Your Name]. How may I assist you today?"
2. Greeting Script (Email)
   - "Dear [Customer's Name], Thank you for reaching out to us at [Company Name]. How can we help you?"
3. Problem Resolution Script
   - Apologize for the issue and assure the customer that you will assist them.
   - Gather all necessary details to understand the problem fully.
   - Offer a solution or propose alternatives.
   - Provide clear instructions or steps to resolve the issue.
   - Thank the customer for bringing the matter to your attention.
4. Complaint Response Email Template
   - Start with a polite greeting and acknowledgment of the customer's complaint.
   - Apologize for the inconvenience caused.
   - Provide an explanation or resolution to address the complaint.
   - Offer any necessary follow-up or compensation, if applicable.
   - Express gratitude for the customer's feedback and their continued support.
5. Thank You Email Template

- Start with a personalized greeting.
- Express gratitude for the customer's business and support.
- Mention specific details of the customer's purchase or interaction.
- Offer any additional assistance or information.
- Close with a warm closing and your contact information.

6. Follow-Up Email Template
- Start with a friendly greeting and mention the previous interaction.
- Express gratitude for the customer's time and feedback.
- Summarize the discussion or action points from the previous conversation.
- Confirm any next steps or timelines.
- Offer your contact information and encourage the customer to reach out with any further questions or concerns.

Customize these scripts and templates to align with your company's tone of voice and branding guidelines. Personalize your customer interactions to build rapport and provide excellent service.

Note: This book serves as a comprehensive guide for individuals starting or scaling a small business. The information provided is based on general principles and may require customization based on specific local regulations and industry requirements. Always consult with legal, financial, and business professionals before making any significant decisions regarding your business.

Appendix F: Research and Industry Articles

These resources include research links, and industry
articles that can provide guidance and support for
entrepreneurs. Whether you need educational materials,
industry insights, or collaboration platforms, these
resources can help you navigate the startup landscape in
San Diego.

Research Links:
- San Diego Regional Economic Development
  Corporation (https://www.sandiegobusiness.org/)
- Small Business Administration (SBA) San Diego
  District Office
  (https://www.sba.gov/offices/district/ca/san-diego)
- San Diego Workforce Partnership
  (https://workforce.org/)

Industry Articles:
- San Diego Union-Tribune Business Section
  (https://www.sandiegouniontribune.com/business)
- San Diego Business Journal
  (https://www.sdbj.com/)
- San Diego Metro Magazine
  (https://sandiegometro.com/)

Note: The availability and suitability of these resources
may vary. It is recommended to verify the details and
requirements of each resource before use.

Appendix G: SBDC Sites

The San Diego & Imperial Valley Small Business Development Centers (SBDC) is a fantastic free resource for any Small Business that seeks advice and support with all the topics covered in this book and much more. From one-on-one coaching to government contract training, they have you covered.

North San Diego SBDC in MiraCosta College:
- https://www.sdivsbdc.org/
- Provides free one-on-one consulting, training programs, and resources for small businesses and startups in North San Diego County.

Imperial Valley SBDC:
- https://www.sdivsbdc.org/
- Offers no-cost consulting services, training programs, and resources to assist entrepreneurs and small businesses in the Imperial Valley region.

East County SBDC - East County Economic Development Council:
- https://eastcountyedc.org/
- Provides business counseling, workshops, and resources to foster economic growth and support startups in East County, San Diego.

South San Diego SBDC in Southwestern Community College:
- https://www.southwesterncollege.edu/sbdc
- Offers no-cost consulting services, training programs, and resources for small businesses and startups in South San Diego County.

Alliance SBDC - Asian Business Association of San Diego:
- https://abasd.org/
- Supports Asian American entrepreneurs and small business owners by providing resources, workshops, and networking opportunities.

The Central San Diego Black Chamber of Commerce:
- https://www.csdbcc.org/

- Promotes the growth and success of Black-owned businesses in Central San Diego through networking events, educational programs, and advocacy.

The San Diego County Imperial Valley Hispanic Chamber of Commerce:
- https://sdihcc.com/
- Supports Hispanic-owned businesses through networking events, business resources, and advocacy in San Diego County and the Imperial Valley.

International Rescue Committee SBDC:
- https://www.rescue.org/united-states/san-diego-ca
- Offers business development services and resources to refugees, immigrants, and low-income individuals in the San Diego area.

The Brink SBDC at the University of San Diego:
- https://www.brinksandiego.org/
- Provides incubation services, mentoring, workshops, and resources to support early-stage startups and entrepreneurs in the San Diego region.

Connect SBDC:
- https://connect.org/
- Offers entrepreneurial training programs, mentoring, and resources to support the growth of technology and life sciences startups in San Diego.

Export SBDC at the World Trade Center San Diego:
- https://www.sdivsbdc.org/
- Assists businesses in expanding into international markets by providing export consulting, trade education, and resources.

Note: It is advisable to visit each website and contact the respective organizations for detailed information about the services, programs, and eligibility criteria they offer.

MIGUEL D. VASQUEZ

Miguel D. Vasquez, an immigrant from Mexico, overcame challenges to become a successful entrepreneur, financial expert, and community advocate. He earned a business administration degree from the University of San Diego where he was recognized with the Bishop Francis Buddy Humanitarian of the Year award. Miguel has held key roles at institutions like HSBC and US Bank, managing retail, small businesses, and premier wealth centers. He has made significant contributions to nonprofit organizations, including his role as a trustee in establishing InterAmerican College (AIC), the founder of the California Foundation Fund (CAFF), and the founder of the Future Boss Youth Entrepreneurship program. As a published contributor to Forbes Magazine, Miguel shares his expertise on finance-related topics. Currently, he supports and empowers small business leaders throughout San Diego, aiming to drive job growth and enhance the quality of life in San Diego County. Miguel's remarkable journey, entrepreneurial skills, and commitment to community service have established him as a highly respected leader in executive leadership, finance, education, small business coaching, and workforce development.

www.ingramcontent.com/pod-product-compliance
Lightning Source LLC
Chambersburg PA
CBHW070917270326
41927CB00011B/2608